Through My Classroom Door

Through My Classroom Door

✦

Edith Bell Poe

iUniverse, Inc.
New York   Bloomington

Through My Classroom Door

iUniverse books may be ordered through booksellers or by contacting:

iUniverse
1663 Liberty Drive
Bloomington, IN 47403
www.iuniverse.com
1-800-Authors (1-800-288-4677)

Because of the dynamic nature of the Internet, any Web addresses or links contained in this book may have changed since publication and may no longer be valid.

ISBN: 978-1-4401-9741-3 (sc)
ISBN: 978-1-4401-9742-0 (ebk)

Library of Congress Control Number: 2010900414

Printed in the United States of America

iUniverse rev. date: 1/29/2010

Contents

Preface

This book is dedicated to all the students who passed through my classroom door. My students' ages ranged from six to fifty-six.

It was my privilege to begin my teaching career in a one-room school. I spent the final twelve years of my career with the Department of Education of the University of Central Oklahoma in Edmond, where I was an assistant professor of reading.

Reading is possibly the most important skill; it is needed for all other subjects. I have found, and still find, the subject challenging. It is a beautiful experience to see anyone, whether six or fifty-six, realize, "I can read!"

Many people made it possible for me to have this wonderful experience. I am thankful to my family, especially my husband, O. Dixon Poe, who encouraged me and gave up his time with me so I could study and attend classes.

I owe a special thank you to Dr. James Morrison, Carrie Chandler Weissinger, Dr. Dale Jordan, Dr. Bette Roberts, Dr. Aaron Dry, Dr. Ernest Jones, and Willie Ingram, my high-school English teacher.

A teacher cannot know how he or she influences a student. Ms. Ingram gave us the objectives for the class. She assured us that if we followed the instructions, there was no reason for failure. I tried to do the same thing for my students.

How many times have I wondered, as I looked at the students sitting in front of me, "Who are you?" Oh, sure, I had their names and information about their families. That is not what I meant.

These students would be with me for only a year. What I wondered was, "Where will your education lead you? Will you be a teacher, doctor, lawyer, engineer, or the CEO of some well-known company? Who are you?"

Once in a while I meet a former student. One of them owns a well-known music store and another one is a teacher. Now and then, someone stares at me with a questioning look that says, "I think I know you." We all change. These people may have been in my classroom.

Hopefully, I played a small part in getting them started down education's road. My goal was to prepare them for the next level of learning.

This book is not fiction. Every incident occurred as it is written. Due to the lapse of time, the names included here may or may not be real.

Chapter 1
The One-room School

My grandson asked my son, "Dad, has Grandmother always been a teacher?" My son told me he had to think about that a bit. Then he replied, "You know, John, she has been a teacher as long as I have known her."

I began teaching when my son was still a baby. He probably cannot remember when I was not a teacher. I have had the rare privilege of teaching from grade one through to the university level. I have met so many wonderful students and many fine parents.

My first school was Soonerville, a one-room school located between the towns of Cushing and Agra in Oklahoma. I learned more in this little one-room school than in all of the years of classes I'd taken for college credit. There were twenty-one students, and all eight grades were represented.

One that first day of school, the students peeked in the door and ran away, laughing, when they saw me sitting at my desk. Curious as I was, I did not ask them why. Much later, when we were well acquainted, one of the boys asked, "Did you wonder why we looked in the classroom and left laughing?"

"Well, yes I did," I said. "Would you like to tell me why you did that?"

Mr. Lowe, a parent and a school board member, had told them that the new teacher was a very big woman, who was really mean, and ate children for breakfast. I am five feet, four inches tall, and at that time I was twenty-two years old and still quite small. The children laughed when they realized that they could hardly see me behind the desk.

What wonderful children they were! Setting aside time for discipline was out of the question. Everyone had to be working while I taught the classes behind the potbellied stove that heated our school. Every minute of the day

1

was needed. I did not want anyone going away without the knowledge he or she needed to move on to the bigger school.

The school board members let the children know that they were completely behind me.

They made a paddle and delivered it to the school while the children watched. They put the paddle in my desk drawer.

There were two precious boys in the first grade. One day when I was teaching history to the eighth grade, these two boys decided to have some fun. We did not have much empty space, but there was some space at the front of the room. These boys thought it would be great fun to fill that area with wads of paper. I saw the first paper wad that was thrown. My first reaction was to stop the boys. Then I remembered that this was my only time for the history class; some subjects, including social studies, civics and science were taught every other day. Everyone knew that I knew what the boys were doing. When the class was over, I walked to my desk and took out my paddle.

I looked at the boys and said, "You had so much fun while I was teaching history. Now it is my turn to have fun. I am going to give each of you swats as long as it takes you to clean up the floor. Bend over."

They did, and I gave them a not-too-hard swat. They ran like little rabbits, cleaning the floor about as fast as they could. Their classmates had a very difficult time holding their laughter. I did not need to give the boys much "encouragement"; they cleaned the room in as little time as possible. That was the only time my paddle came out of the desk drawer.

The first of my students to become ill got the mumps. I had never had the mumps, so I really did not want any contact with this young man. He sent me a bouquet of flowers that he had picked. I was actually afraid to touch them, but I did anyway. He sent me more and more flowers until he recovered from his illness. Apparently, the flowers were not contagious, so I did not need to worry. When you are the only teacher and finding substitutes is next to impossible, you do not want to take a chance.

The one-room school had some advantages. On some of the very cold days we cooked a hot meal; usually this was done with the help of a parent. The children learned from each other. They rapidly became aware of "cause and effect." A good example occurred at lunchtime. In good weather, the children ate outside. The rules were that they were to respect each other and keep the schoolyard free of trash. A fourth-grade boy threw paper on the ground as a "let's test the teacher" act. When I went outside to see how things were going, I saw the paper. I did not ask, "Who did this?" Instead, I picked up the paper and put it in the waste can. It was time for lunch to be over anyway. When everyone was in place, I said, "Someone doesn't want us to have a clean place to eat and play. If this ever happens again, I will ring the bell, and we will start classes immediately. Do all of you understand what I have said?"

The next day, the boy did the same thing. The children surrounded him. They made him pick up his trash. It was all done very quietly and quickly. No one was hurt. He had learned his lesson.

I learned things, too. It was at Soonerville that I learned how to have a "pie supper." One-room schools often held these events to raise money for supplies the budget did not cover. If you have never experienced a pie supper, you cannot imagine how much fun people had. Parents and friends of the school district provided an auctioneer. The ladies made the pies and decorated boxes to hold them. Everyone tried to make a prettier box than anyone else. Then we auctioned off the pies. The highest bidder won the pie and the right to share it with its baker. This gave the entire community the opportunity to get together and have a bit of fun.

My husband was working on his bachelor's degree. He would leave me at Soonerville in the early morning, then travel to Stillwater for an eight o'clock class. He also served as a minister for the Chandler and Davenport Presbyterian churches. This meant that I was a new teacher, a fairly new mother, and a new minister's wife. The stress caused me to lose the use of my left arm, and I had to carry my left arm in a sling for a short time. To the children, this seemed like an excellent time to test the teacher. A sixth-grade boy named Kenneth decided to misbehave. He did not do anything really bad, but he was annoying nonetheless.

We were having an opening exercise. This included saluting the flag and singing a song. It was also a time for the children to talk about things concerning the day or just things of interest to all of us. Billy Joe, an eighth-grade boy, asked for permission to speak. He said, "Mrs. Poe, we do not feel that Kenneth is being fair to you. He knows that you cannot paddle him. You just give us the word, and we will do it for you."

I was watching Kenneth. He looked frightened and seemed to get smaller as I looked at him. I thanked the class for their concern and said, "I have the feeling that Kenneth will not need paddling. He is going to behave."

Many, many years later I learned that Kenneth got his paddling on the way home. The children walked home together, and they took care of business when no one was around to stop them. I had no more trouble from Kenneth.

One day, we had an unexpected visit from the county superintendent. The students sat like little statues and did not participate in the lesson. I could not believe what I was seeing.

When the county superintendent left, I asked, "Now, why did you behave that way?" I laughed because it was so amusing.

One of the students said. "The other teachers told us that we should do that. We were to be very quiet and still while he was here. "I told them they should have kept on doing whatever they were doing. The superintendent wanted to see them at work.

We had a good time together. The opening exercise was a time for sharing. We sang together. We saluted the flag, and then we talked. One of the students surprised me when he told me how much he enjoyed that time together. He said, "We like to joke, but we know when we have gone too far."

"Oh, and how do you know that?"

He said, "When your black eyes snap, we know it is time to stop."

All eight grades were represented during my first year of teaching. Sometimes new teachers learn the hard way. One day, I decided to let all of the grades practice math by adding columns of numbers as fast as possible. This seemed like a great plan until I realized that I did not have an answer book. I managed easily enough until I got to the fifth grade and beyond. I was completely exhausted by the time I reached the end of this experience. The students thoroughly enjoyed the event. We did similar exercises throughout the school year but with only one or two classes at a time.

Today, children are assigned different teachers for different subjects. Most children probably can handle this, but others need the close relationship that occurs when there is only one teacher. The teacher understands when Bobby seems unusually sleepy. She knows a bit about his family background. She recognizes that Bobby's dad has been drinking again and that Bobby's home life has been disrupted by his Dad's unruly behavior. She can be more understanding when his eyes are about to close. She might even encourage him to him to nap a little.

After several months, my husband was ready to move on to a seminary in Chicago. That meant that I had only one year with those wonderful children.

Many years later, my husband and I were in a bowling alley in Edmond, Oklahoma, competing with another couple. The lady said, "You know, I once had a teacher named Mrs. Poe."

"Really," I replied. "Where was that?"

She answered, "It was in a one-room school out near Agra, Oklahoma."

I asked, "Would that school have been Soonerville?"

She smiled. "Yes, it was." I told her that I was that Mrs. Poe. We had a great time reminiscing.

She may have been the student who spent a night with us in our home in Chandler, Oklahoma. She had such beautiful hair. That night she bathed and washed her hair. It's possible that I fixed her hair for her. I certainly enjoyed working with my own hair.

It is really a small world. By this time, I was teaching reading in the Department of Education at the University of Central Oklahoma. One of the ladies working in a store in the Student Union Building asked if I was the Mrs. Poe who taught at Soonerville. I told her that I was and that it had been my first year of teaching. She was the daughter of one of the school board members who had hired me.

I thought back to the day of my interview. I had not had the chance to look for a job until July. By then, the only school with an opening was Soonerville. My husband and I drove out to the community to keep an appointment with the three gentlemen who comprised the school board. I was twenty-two years old. Mr. Lowe, the chairman of the board, said, "Golly gee, we do need a teacher, but we had hoped to find one with some experience." That made me angry because I had worked so very hard to get a degree.

I replied, "And just how do you think I will get experience if I cannot get a job?"

He laughed as he answered, "Lady, you have a job!" I have said it before, but this was a wonderful experience in my teaching career. I learned more in that one year than I did in all of the years I attended college.

Soonerville School

First Graders

More First Graders

Chapter 2
Teaching First Grade

First Graders are so special. The first graders I taught did not have the advantage of daycare or kindergarten. They came right from home to school.

Lindsey was so frightened of the first day of school. She did not sleep well because she was worrying about not knowing "how to spell." Her mother came to me and asked if she might stay for a while. I assured her that she was welcome, and that she could come to my class anytime she wished. She took a seat at the back of the room. We started the day by singing, "Good Morning to You" and saluting the flag. The song goes like this:

Good morning to you.
Good morning to you
We are all in our places with sunshiny faces.
Oh, this is the way to start a new day.

Next, I asked the students to play some "finger stories" with me. The first one was "Ten Little Squirrels"; we used our fingers to portray the actions of the squirrels. It went like this:

"Put your arms together to make a tree. Spread your fingers out to make the limbs. Now follow me. The first two squirrels said, 'What do we see?' The second two squirrels said, 'A man with a gun!' The third two squirrels said, 'Let's run! Let's run!' The fourth two squirrels said, 'Let's hide in the shade!' The fifth two squirrels said, 'Awe, we are not afraid!' Bang went the gun and away the squirrels did run!"

I placed the printed names of the children around the room and asked each one to find his or her name. This allowed them to get out of their seats and move around. By this time, the children were ready to start the new school year. Lindsey went to the back of the room and dismissed her mother. Everything was going to be okay.

Later, when I was teaching at the University of Central Oklahoma, one of those former first graders visited me. She told me that she had been upset because I did not spell her complete name that first day of school. Her name was Montressa Jo, but I had written her name as Monte Jo; that was what she was usually called.

Judy always arrived in tears. Her father would bring her to school. She would kiss him goodbye and burst into tears. One day I asked, "Do you not like to come to school?" She answered, "No, I like school." So I asked, "Then why do you cry every morning as you leave your dad?" She shrugged and said, "I don't know."

I decided that crying was something she felt she should do so her dad would know that she missed him. I asked her to play a game with me. The next morning, she would kiss her dad goodbye, smile, and say, "I will see you after school." Then she should leave with a smile on her face. She did this. I saw her dad wipe away his tears. His little girl had made the break from baby to "little lady."

It was enrollment day for first grade. I watched as Sarah entered the room with her mother, who stopped to visit with another parent. Sarah came to my table. I asked, "Would you like to start enrolling while you wait for your mother?" Sarah said she would like that. When we reached the part of the form that listed the parents, she said, "We are divorced, you know." I replied, "No, I did not know. I am sorry. Would you like for me to include your father?" She nodded yes.

Much later in the year, I saw Sarah carefully studying me. I wondered what was on her mind. Then she slid out of her desk and started toward my desk. Sometimes we do things that we do not understand. I turned my chair and opened my arms to Sarah. She crawled into my lap and put her head on my shoulder. Neither of us spoke. She was not there long. She looked at me and said, "Now, I can work."

Today, there are so many rules restricting teachers from showing children that they are loved. This experience would not now be possible. It was all right for Sarah to come into my arms and know that she was loved. Now that I think back about it, the miracle was that I did not have to give equal time to each of the thirty children in that class. Don't laugh; I am very serious. For example, I have a habit of placing a pencil behind my ear. Imagine my surprise to see all of my first graders with a pencil behind an ear. It was so funny that I burst out laughing. They laughed with me, and we all removed our pencils. Other teachers will find that their students will mimic them just as mine copied me.

An apple for the teacher was a way to show her how special she was to a particular student. Sam brought a very shiny apple and placed it on my desk. "Oh, my!" I said. "How did you get that apple so shiny?" Sam picked up the apple and started rubbing it up and down his pant leg. He said, "Just like this."

Then there was Joe and his gift of an apple. I knew that Joe did not come from a wealthy family. He proudly placed an apple on my desk. "Thank you, Joe," I said. "Are you sure that you do want that apple for your lunch?" Joe answered, "No, I want you to have it." Then at recess Joe stopped at my desk, took the apple in his hands, and grabbed a quick bite. He put it back on my desk.

Imagine my surprise when, many years later, one of my university students placed a beautiful apple on my desk. She smiled and said, "We have a basket of apples, and they are so good. I just could not resist bringing one to you." So you see, apples and teachers just go together.

It was time for the Christmas program at Oak Park School. The first grade had the responsibility for that year's program. We worked with the music teacher to make it special. Then our Santa Claus came down with the chicken pox. We had to choose another Santa Claus. We chose Teddy. We gathered everything for the program and marched down the long hall to the auditorium. It was then that I realized that we did not have the Santa suit. I asked Teddy to run back to the room and see if we had left the suit there. Teddy ran to the room and came back. He said, "Yes, we left the Santa suit in the room." I burst out laughing because Teddy had done exactly what I had told him to do. Now I said, "Would you please hurry to the room and bring the Santa suit to me?"

I was still laughing as Teddy hurried to return the Santa suit to me. The principal approached me as asked, "What happened?" I told him that Teddy had done exactly what I requested. After all, I had not told him to bring the Santa suit.

That year, the curriculum included teaching "Economy Phonics." We had a wonderful time together working through the exercises. First, we learned the long vowel sounds and then the short vowel sounds. There was always a list of words at the bottom of the page. These were for additional practice in using the newly learned sound. We busily worked through the words.

We were studying the short u sound. The next word was "but." A doctor's son said, "Umm, that is not a nice word." The superintendent's son replied, "Well, that depends. If you say, 'I wanted to go to the show, but my mother would not let me,' that's all right. Now if you are talking about your 'behind,' that is another matter." This was very serious philosophizing for first graders. I had to make myself very busy at the blackboard to keep myself under control.

The principal asked me to teach a demonstration class in front of the local Lion's Club.

I told him I would be happy to do this if the class could be a regular class. He agreed. I had no idea how my first graders would react to all of this attention. When the time came, we acknowledged the men and proceeded with the lesson.

The first graders seemed not even to know the men were watching. Everyone participated will full attention through the class. The men clapped, and some of them came to thank us for being there. One gentleman asked, "Now. How come the teachers didn't teach like that when I attended school?"

I saw Bill on the day the first grade was enrolling. We had two first-grade classes, so I hoped Bill would be in the other one. Well, he wasn't. The classes were divided according to age, and I had chosen to take the younger group, which included Bill. He was a positively handsome youngster and as bright as he could be, but he had a mischievous streak. The very first day of school, he put me to the test. It was my turn to be on duty during the recess period.

Our school had a beautiful building; the playground was surrounded by the classrooms. This made it a safe place, except for Bill, who placed himself at the drinking fountain so he could spray water at the other children. I said, "Bill, get your drink and move away from the fountain."

He quickly retorted, "Shut up, you idiot!" Again I demanded, "Get your drink and move away from the fountain!" Bill did not hesitate. Again he shouted, "And I said, shut up, you idiot!"

This time I walked over where he was and took his hand and led him into our classroom. When we were inside, I said, "Bill, I am very angry. You had better take your seat while I calm down and then we need to have a talk. Do you understand!" He agreed and went to his seat. That was encouraging. I had thought he might give me trouble with that request. We sat calmly, just looking at each other. Then I called him over so we could talk. I said, "Bill, this is you first year to attend school. There are many things you must learn, and one of the first is that you mind your teacher. You never ever even call your best friend an idiot, and you certainly do not call your teacher an idiot!" He looked at me and asked, "Then, how come my daddy calls my mom an idiot?" I told him that I did not know why his daddy would do such a thing. I could not tell his parents how to talk, but I could insist that he treat everyone at school with respect.

That was an interesting year. Bill was not a bad child, but he was mischievous. That was the only time my first graders knew exactly who had taken their missing pencil or crayons. Instead of complaining to me they would look at Bill and say, "Okay, Bill, what did you do with them?"

All of the teachers knew Bill. The school year was ending, and I was having lunch with the teachers. I said, "Ladies, Bill soon will be a second grader. Which one of you lucky people are going to get him?" We all had a big laugh. Bill would be a challenge because he faced many challenges at home.

This school was located in a rather wealthy area, so it was a surprise when little Shirley showed up. I was so glad Shirley was in my class. I knew what it was to have little in the way of material possessions. Shirley was supposed to be blonde, but her hair was so dirty you really could not tell it. Her clothes were worn and unkempt. Shirley was really a very brave little girl. She didn't seem to notice that she was different. The other children treated her well. I would have seen to it that they did, if it had been necessary.

My first grade presented the PTA program one day. The parents always turned out for these programs. A judge's wife asked, "Isn't there anything we can do for that poor little girl?" I told her I had been trying to think of something. I had considered buying her some clothes, but they would just get dirty. Her appearance would not change. I had already asked Shirley to come early so I could bathe her face and brush her hair. The little girl was pleased with the extra attention I gave her.

The judge's wife asked me to let her work things out. She came with clothes for six days. She had everything from underwear to a nice coat. We decided that I would change Shirley before the children arrived and keep her long enough after school to change her into her own clothes. This wonderful lady picked up Shirley's dirty clothes and returned the laundered ones to the school each week. Oh, yes, Shirley had new shoes and socks, too.

You could see Shirley's self-esteem rise. She became our little Cinderella. The girls caught on and begged to help Shirley dress for the day and put on her clothes at the end of the day. We set up a schedule so they could take turns.

Shirley's parents never came to the school or acted as though they had any knowledge of what was happening. The clothes were all given to Shirley at the end of the year.

Little Bruce was severely handicapped with rheumatoid arthritis. The arthritis had stunted his growth but not his mind. He was very intelligent and did some of the best work in the class. His fingers were curled, but he still had the best handwriting. He motivated the rest of the class to try harder to make their work pretty. We often had to call his parents to come and take him home or bring him medicine when the pain became too difficult.

Children can be cruel when someone is different, no matter what the reason. It was such a pleasure, however, to see the other children interact with Bruce. He participated in any activity on the playground. When recess was over and the bell rang, signaling the children to line up, they always ran. It didn't matter how many times you reminded them that it was not necessary to run. It was wonderful to see a boy let Bruce get ahead of him. I heard this boy say, "Boy, Bruce, I did not know you could run that fast!" The beautiful smile on Bruce's face was reward enough.

I was fortunate to teach at a time when discipline was not difficult. The students often handled situations themselves. The desks were arranged side by side. The girl sitting next to Bruce had her hair in long pigtails. She dropped her crayons on the floor. She bent over to pick them up and swatted Bruce with her hair. He just glared at her. Down she went again and again. Each time she swatted Bruce with her hair. Finally, Bruce hit her with his pencil. She glared at him and said something that I could not hear. Down she went and swatted Bruce with her hair. Again, Bruce hit her with his pencil. This time she got the message. She was more careful in gathering the rest of her crayons. I saw everything. They did not need my help in handling the problem.

It was time for school pictures. The students were to bring money before pictures were ordered. A picture with all of the students was on the bulletin board with lines below for the names of those placing orders. Bruce's mother stopped by the classroom during that time. She asked, "Didn't Bruce bring his money?" I told her no. When I asked him he said that their three children just kept them broke. She laughed. "That little rascal. He has lost his money and doesn't want to tell us." She gave me the money for his picture.

Laura was so tiny. This petite girl wore glasses that seemed large on her face. I knew that Laura could read the day she arrived. She did not tell me. This school had a supervisor who insisted on several weeks, I cannot remember how many, of readiness for reading training. Laura entered into all of the activities without any indication of boredom. The other students did the same activities with enthusiasm. I kept reminding them that in a few days they would get their first books. You cannot imagine how thrilled they were to be given the first of several pre-primers.

I took Laura aside. I told her that I knew she could read, but that the school insisted that she had to read the same pre-primers as the other students. I turned to the back of the book and had her read the word list. She zipped through without a mistake. I had her read the first book.

I called Laura's parents and asked for a conference. I told them that we had a problem. It was more of an opportunity than a problem, but I needed their help. I told them that I intended to turn Laura loose in reading. They were to get library cards, and Laura and I would do the same. When the mobile library came around each month, we all would check out books for Laura to read. These books would become her reading texts after she had completed the regular first grade readers.

Laura listened to her parents as they talked about a lady named Cynthia. She said, "I can spell that." The she spelled s-y-n-t-h-i-a. Her mother said, "No, that is not correct. C-y-n-t-h-i-a is the correct spelling." Laura stomped her foot and asked, "How can you tell a soft c from a hard c? Laura's mother asked, "Do you teach her those rules?" I told her that I did. It was important that the students had help in dealing with new words.

The next day I reminded the class that the soft 'c' sounded like an 's'. The soft c sounded like an s. The soft c was usually followed by an e, i, or y. This rule works most of the time.

Laura was not ahead in writing skills, math, or any other subject other than reading, so she worked with the rest of the class in those areas. She was always an eager learner. The second-grade teacher said, "Don't you dare give her the second-grade reader." I replied, "Don't worry. That would be holding her back."

Laura had been ill. She returned to school, but she was not ready to go outside and play.

She stayed in the room and read. I had hall duty that day. I asked her if she would like to sit with me. She took her book and read as I watched the hall. Some sixth-grade girls passed by and noticed the book she was reading. They were whispering as they moved away. I said, "She is not in trouble. She has been ill and needs to stay inside." One of the girls asked, "Is she reading that book?" I turned to Laura and asked, "Are you reading 'The Pink Hotel'?" She nodded. I asked the girls if they wanted to hear her read. They said they would, and Laura read for them. They thanked her and moved on down the hall. I overheard one of them saying, "She can read better than I can."

At the end of the year, Laura tested at the sixth-grade level in reading. She was also an excellent speller.

One day, my husband and I were leaving a baseball game early so we would not have to cope with the traffic. By this time, I was teaching at the University of Central Oklahoma. I heard a gasp and a voice. "Mother, that is Mrs. Poe." I stopped, and Laura came running to me. We had a wonderful reunion. Every teacher should experience teaching a Laura.

First graders can be cruel. Tim had an ugly sore on his cheek. It was the type of sore that needed air so it was not covered with a bandage. The class was exiting the door for recess. Jerry pointed to Tim's sore and yelled, "Look at Tim! See the sore on his face! Ha, ha, ha." Tim began crying. I called both boys to me. I said, "Jerry, I want you to play a game with me. Just for a moment I want you to be the boy with the ugly sore on your face. Tim, I want you to yell for your classmates to look at Jerry's face and repeat the things Jerry said about you."

Then I looked at Jerry and asked, "Now, how do you feel?" Jerry started crying. "There is no need for tears. I believe you understand that what you did was wrong. What Tim needs is a friend who will take him by the hand and play with him." Jerry stretched out his hand and took Tim's, and they dashed off laughing. They became good friends after that little episode.

On National Education Day, the students displayed their work for their parents. Each teacher did something unique for the occasion. I decided to let each child make a paper doll representing herself or himself. I traced the child's outline on a piece of butcher paper. We worked on these each day during our art class. We had plenty of room for each child to work. It was such a surprise when a beautiful little redhead colored her hair black. I asked, "Why did you decide to become a brunette?" She answered, "I like black hair, so I painted my hair black."

Who knows why she did it? My hair was black, but I have no idea what prompted her to change her hair color.

Another afternoon, when the children were working, I heard a scream. I went to see what was wrong. The girl was almost in tears. She said, "I cut my head off!" I told her, "Don't you worry, I will help you repair your doll. You don't need to start over."

We placed these life-size paper dolls in the children's seats. A special booklet with each student's work was on the desk in front of the doll. The parents were delighted.

George was another of those intelligent but spoiled children. He had three older sisters who jumped at his beck and call. His parents were good people who wanted to rear their children correctly.

I met George when I was teaching an ungraded primary class in Oklahoma City school. One day, George started to leave the room. I stopped him and asked, "Where are you going?"

He answered, "I am going to the hallway."

"I don't remember anything being said about you going to the hallway. Where did you get this idea?"

He said, "Well, all of the other teachers sent me to the hallway."

I replied, "George, you have just graduated from the hallway. When you think you just must get away from the class, take your chair and sit in the corner. That way you won't miss your classwork. Then when you are ready you may bring your chair and join us. You may not go back to your seat."

This became something all of us—students and teacher—understood. Every now and then, we would see George pick up his chair and head for the corner of the classroom. When he became interested in what we were doing, he would bring his chair and join us.

I spent lots of time walking from recess with my arms around George's shoulder, explaining to him that it was not necessary for him to always be first in line. Teaching him to share "rainy day games and toys" was a challenge. One rainy day, I had hall duty. My students had access to a collection of toys for these days. I could always watch them from the hallway. George was making a concerted effort to share. It was not easy for him. He was accustomed to doing whatever pleased him. He grimaced as he let another student have a toy that he wanted. I smiled as George relinquished the toy. I considered this to be progress.

After I left that school, I would be driving in Oklahoma City, and some young man would go racing past me as I drove the speed limit. A thought would pop into my mind: *That must be George. He always wants to be first.*

We all contributed to a "Writing Book." Each child could choose whatever he or she wished to be his or her story for the day. I would spell any word that they could not. The criteria for stories included in our Writing Book were neatness and an appropriate subject. I usually chose several, and the children voted on their inclusion in our book. No one was excluded, but not everyone was included every day. The stories could be illustrated or not illustrated. One day, George asked how to spell "sexy." I spelled it for him. That day his story was not included in our book, so he took the paper home. I had a call from his mother. She wanted a conference. When we met, she asked, "What did you think about George including the word 'sexy' in his story?" I replied, "Oh, I just thought George had heard a word that he thought might stir up a little excitement." His mother gasped. "Why didn't I talk with you before I sent him to his father?"

George was an excellent student. Today, he is probably an executive somewhere.

The school principal liked our creative writing. She would stop by to see the new additions. Our book was displayed so the children could enjoy the stories, too. On the last day of school, the principal came in and picked up our Writing Book. She said, "Class, this is my keepsake of this class." I was surprised, and the class was quite pleased.

Randy was the baby of the family. His mother was very protective, to the point of being overprotective. The first day of school, she sat in her car for a long time before leaving. Randy was aware that she was there. He was afraid because usually he was not permitted to do anything outside of his mother's presence. This situation continued until I knew that I had to do something.

I asked Randy if he had a picture of his mother. He said that he did. I suggested that he bring it to school and keep it where he could look at it. That would be like having her there.

Oddly enough, this little ploy worked. Randy adjusted and became the wonderful student I knew he could be. It was a bit harder for his mother to let go.

I met some of my first graders when I started a tutoring program at the Bella Vista Community Church. Kenny was one of those children. Kenny's tutor was absent and, since I was the director and filled in whenever needed, I knew Kenny. He was a joy and caught everyone's attention. He loved coming to tutoring because he had an adult's total attention. He would come in and sort of wander around, looking to see what everyone was doing. At that time, we were all spread out in the rather large overflow room.

I told him that I was his tutor for that day. He seemed so happy and ready to work. I said, "You must have had a wonderful day at school today." Wow! That was the wrong thing to say. He shook his head and seemed ready to cry.

He said, "No, I didn't! It has been an awful day!"

I asked, "Would you like to talk about it?"

"I guess so," he answered.

"What is bothering you?" I asked.

"Well, I just get into trouble all of the time!" he said.

"Really? Where do you get into trouble?"

"Everywhere!"

I said, "Suppose that we take one place at a time. Where would you like to start?"

Kenny looked so sad and said, "Let's start with the school bus."

"Fine," I replied. "What happened on the school bus?"

He started, "You know, I really like the bus driver, but I still do things I know he doesn't want me to do."

"Such as?" I asked.

"Oh, I get out of my seat. I yell, and I start trouble."

"If you are not pleased with what you do, is there anything you can do about it?"

"Yeah," Kenny answered. "I know what to do. I just have not been doing it."

"You will solve most of the problems when you are willing to look at them with an open mind. So what is the solution?"

Kenny smiled, "I know! I am going to tell the bus driver that I am sorry. Then I am going to kiss him and go to my seat and behave!"

"That sounds just about perfect," I replied. "Where do we go next?"

Kenny was thoughtful. "How about my classroom?"

"That's fine with me," I said. "What is wrong there?"

"I don't get my work done. I like to get up and walk around the room and stuff like that," he answered.

"So, how can you correct things there?" I asked.

He looked quite serious. "Well, I can do my work, I can stay in my seat, and things like that."

"That sounds good to me. Do you have some other problems?" I asked.

"Yes!" Kenny quickly answered. "I get in trouble at home."

"In what way do you get into trouble at home?"

Kenny was still very serious. " I lie a lot," he confessed.

"And that bothers you?"

"Yes!"

"What is the solution there?" I asked.

He straightened up his shoulders and smiled. "I will tell the truth, and I will do what I am supposed to do!"

"Do you feel better now?" I asked. He nodded and smiled. At that point, we began the work he had come to do.

When I tell Kenny's story, I wonder how many other children are walking through life just wishing someone would listen to them.

Adam's mother came to the church tutoring program almost in tears. She said, "My son is not learning to read. Can you help him?" I assured her that we would try. Adam was severely dyslexic. It was my privilege to tackle this problem. Adam was a beautiful child in every way. He had a wonderful attitude and was so handsome. Adam had seen his home life change. His parents were divorced, and it was having an effect on him.

We started at the beginning. He responded well to one-on-one attention. I used a linguistic form of phonics. We worked on word parts to which he responded vocally. He enjoyed this. It was like a game. The words were also his spelling words. He had his own workbook, and his good work was rewarded with funny stickers. We read out loud every day.

Sometimes I would ask him to put a marker under the line and guide me while I did the oral reading. Then he read the same passage. It did not matter that he sometimes memorized the paragraph. He was learning the vocabulary. He increased his repertoire of words, which helped with anything else he read. I also used the repeated reading method to teach Adam. We would reread the same passage during each class until he could read it without mistakes. Sometimes I would ask Adam to tell me about something he enjoyed. I wrote as he talked, and then had him read his own story. We made a book of Adam's stories. Changes slowly took place. He fairly beamed as he arrived for tutoring. He improved slowly, but the school noticed the change. He was moved from the mentally retarded class to the learning disabled class. His mother told us he was so much happier, and so was she. Adam eventually moved away, but he was learning and that was what was important.

One day the Bella Vista Community Church minister and secretary were in the tutoring area. This was unusual. The secretary said, "We will keep you posted on what is happening."

That was just fine, but I had no idea anything was wrong. I asked what she meant. She said we were under a tornado alert. It was time for the classes to begin, and a group of children from the schools in Gravette, Arkansas, arrived. A little later, the volunteer receptionist said Adam's grandfather had called to say that he would pick up Adam. Oh, my! Where was Adam? I felt a tug on my sleeve, and there was Adam. "Where have you been?" I asked. "Well, there's been a tornado, you know," said Adam. "The bus had to go around trees. Sometimes we had to move some of them." Someone asked where Adam's tutor was. I replied, "Anyone who had to go to that much trouble to get to class has a tutor. I will be his tutor." Right then Adam's grandfather appeared, so the boy did not have a tutoring lesson that day.

A member of our church sensed that I knew how to teach reading. Her son was in the first grade. She was so worried about him. He was in the Sparrow's Group. Now, everyone knows that the sparrow is a very common bird, so she naturally determined that her son was in the lowest group. I never named reading groups, but I knew that many teachers did.

Bobby came to my home twice a week. I knew after the first lesson that Bobby had to be doing well in school. "Have you visited with the teacher?" I asked his mother. "No, but I don't need to," she said. "If he is a Sparrow, he has to be in the lowest group." I insisted that she visit the school and see the situation for herself. She did. She called me and was laughing as she told me that, sure enough, Bobby was in the top reading group. In fact, Bobby was the only boy in the top reading group. Girls mature faster than boys. It was not unusual for girls to be ahead in reading. Bobby was doing just fine.

So you see, even Sparrows can fly!

Bobby's mother insisted that we continue the lessons anyway. He enjoyed coming, and I enjoyed teaching him. His mother and I traded work for work. She was an excellent seamstress. My daughter was taking dance lessons and needed special costumes. This was a solution for both of us.

I met another first grader under similar circumstances. He was younger than most of his class. He was struggling. His mother pleaded with me to take him after school. Jimmy was happy to have my attention. I used the Economy Phonics system. He took to this like a duck to water. It was a game. We always did phonics and oral reading. Later, I started teaching comprehension skills. His teacher was singing a different song. The teacher said Jimmy was so far ahead of the class, she was pleading with the mother to stop the lessons. Of course, she didn't.

Julie was the youngest of a family with adult children. She had learned how to manage all of them. Her parents were devastated when Julie's teacher called them for a conference. The teacher announced that the parents should be prepared for Julie to repeat first grade because she simply would be too immature to move up to the second grade in one year. The teacher and a counselor made this judgment at the beginning of the school year in September. I could not believe that I had heard correctly. I had taught for too many years to accept that opinion. Children mature a great deal in one year. And I knew that Julie was intelligent.

Julie's parents pleaded with me, "Please tutor Julie two times a week, and we will both tutor other children." That was a bargain because we needed more tutors. Julie became my student.

Experience had taught me that a child like Julie must be put in a situation with no distractions. Our teaching table was placed against the wall. Julie sat next to the wall, and I sat beside her. She was eager to learn. I used the Glass Analysis word clusters to teach her both word sounds and spelling. Dr. Gerald Glass and his wife had found an effective way to teach people how to read by focusing on recognizable groups of letters in words. They called their system Glass Analysis. We studied "sight words" ten at a time. These words were printed on plain index cards and placed before her. We said the words together several times. Then I would shuffle the cards and ask her to tell me the words. She would pick up a card and say the word. She placed an X on the back of the words she said correctly. During the next lesson, we repeated these words. Again she placed an X on the back of the cards she could remember. Three Xs meant that word belonged to her, and she could take that card home. New words replaced the conquered words.

We always read aloud. I used the same methods that had worked for Adam. Julie was so happy that she could read. Her teacher and counselor were so certain that she would fail that they withheld the school readers from her. I told her she would be able to read anything in the textbooks.

The next year, her parents transferred her to another school. We received a wonderful thank you card from her family. It said that Julie was at the head of her class.

Jane came to school with one of her baby teeth barely holding on. She would not let her mother pull the tooth. She wanted her teacher to pull it. I did, and she was so proud of herself for being brave. We wrapped the tooth safely so she could take it home and the tooth fairy could find it under her pillow. Who knew what the tooth fairy might leave in exchange for the treasured tooth!

When I was a child, storms terrified me. I would put a pillow over my head so I could not see the lightning, even though I could still hear the thunder that followed. After I was married, my wonderful husband would put his arms around me and explain what was happening.

He told me about the warm air and the cold air coming together. He explained that lightning did wonderful things for the soil. The storms were still terrifyingly awesome, but I understood more about them. I still respected the danger as well as the good.

One day, a horrible thunderstorm came in the middle of the day. My first graders kept working, but they were watching me. I reminded myself that I could not show fear. If I did, I would have a big problem on my hands.

Sammy tiptoed to my desk and whispered, "I am not afraid of the storm here. Why am I so afraid at home?"

We had a very large book exhibited on a bulletin board. We read a page out loud each day. My first graders felt that they were reading even though we read the book together. This was part of the readiness program, which ensured that the children were prepared to start school.

Another first grader joined our Bella Vista Community Church tutoring program at midterm. Henry was younger than the other first graders, and readiness was his main problem. Sylvia, a wonderfully patient tutor, became Henry's tutor. She worked diligently through the sight word list. She listened to him read each day. Henry became a good reader. He bounced into the room one afternoon with a big smile and announced, "I am the best reader in my class!"

I challenged him. "Who says so?" He did not hesitate as he answered, "My teacher says so!"

We all laughed, and I said, "That is good enough for me."

Sylvia took her excited Henry to begin lessons. He was fairly zipping through the reading. Sylvia worried about his level of comprehension. She stopped him now and then to ask a question. Henry grew serious and looked at her. Sylvia asked, "Henry, what are you thinking?" He quickly answered, "You know, if you did not ask so many questions, we could finish this book."

I wanted to teach the concept of left and right. The children were in a circle around the room and we did the hokey pokey. Children react to rhythm and music so naturally, this seemed like a good idea. I told them to follow me. "Put your right hand in. Put your right hand out, and shake it all about. Now do the hokey pokey, and turn yourself about." We did this with the left hand, the right foot, and the left foot. The children loved it.

Guess what? The teacher was called on the carpet for teaching the children to dance. So much for using that technique to teach right and left.

Janet was attending a class for teachers who were finding out how to deal with learning problems. I was working with her that day. Everything was moving along just fine. She looked at me and said, "I really don't like that dark lipstick you are wearing today."

"I am sorry about that," I said. "The next time we work together, I will not wear that color." She seemed satisfied, so we continued the lesson.

Mrs. Michener was a first-grade teacher in another school. A boy named Joe had been disobedient. She asked him, "What do you think I should do with you? You knew you would get into trouble." Joe answered, "I think you should paddle me." Mrs. Michener replied, "Now, why should I do that? You know where the paddle is. Paddle yourself." Joe walked to the desk, picked up the paddle and proceeded to spank himself. He cried. Mrs. Michener said, "That should be enough. See that you behave yourself. Do you understand?" Joe stopped crying and agreed that he could obey.

Another first-grade boy looked at Mrs. Michener and said, "Oh, you have the most beautiful eyes!" Mrs. Michener said, "Why thank you!" The boy continued, "They are just like old Bossey's."

Schools in Woodward, Oklahoma, gave teachers a day to attend a special program in another school district. A parent served as a substitute. Judith's mother was the substitute the day the reports were received about an eye exam. That day she learned that her beautiful brilliant little daughter had sight in only one eye. She said, "If you had been here we would have cried together." And we would have. Her daughter was one of the top students in the class.

I first met Sabra when her family moved to our town and came to our church. She was so beautiful, but she was larger than most six-year olds. Her parents joined our church and brought along their precious daughter and son. They asked for a conference. Sabra had been a normal child until a mysterious illness sent her into a high fever, which left her brain damaged. She had learned to defend herself by grabbing her opponents and choking them. She had been refused admittance to other schools. The parents wanted to know if I would accept her in my first grade.

I agreed to give her a chance. My first effort was to get her to sit with me in church. She was delighted that someone besides her parents wanted to be close to her. She handled church well.

Then it was time to test her ability to work with others in the classroom.

Sabra enrolled in my first-grade class. I kept close watch on her interactions with the other students. It was obvious that she could not do the classwork. The association with others would be the main part of her learning. She tried. She would copy what was on the board. She would mimic the other children.

We had our own private restroom. One day Sabra locked herself in the restroom. This terrified me. I had to get the janitor to let me in. I scolded Sabra and told her not to do that again. Those were wasted words. Later she locked herself in the restroom again. I asked the rest of the class to play a game with me.

I explained that Sabra locked herself in the restroom in an effort to get attention. When she returned to the classroom, could they pretend that she had never left? They agreed that they would all be busy when she returned. In this way, we ignored her effort to frighten us. Soon we heard the restroom door opening. The students were very busy with their work, and I kept writing on the blackboard. Sabra went to her desk. She looked at me. Then she looked at her classmates. It was amazing to see how the class managed to keep busy and pay her no attention.

She took out paper and pencil and tried to copy what I was writing. Thus her effort to scare us by locking herself in the restroom came to an end.

I talked with specialists to get recommendations for working with Sabra. Paddling was suggested. I would not and could not even consider that suggestion. I did put a ruler on my desk. Someone somewhere had used a ruler on her. When she was misbehaving, all I had to do was pick up the ruler. She would say, "No, I will be good."

Sabra tried playing with the other children, who accepted her limitations. It was touching when she came running to me and said, "I love you." I hugged her and said, "I love you too."

She would run back to play with the other children.

We made it through the year. Her parents decided to put her in a boarding school for the severely handicapped.

Becky's mother came to my home. Pretty, brown-eyed little Becky was with her. Something was obviously wrong. I invited them in, but the mother said she'd rather not enter the house because she thought that Becky had a contagious infection. She asked me to look at Becky's beautiful brown hair.

There, at the tip of the forehead, was a large sore. I told her mother that it looked like ringworm and asked if she had seen a doctor. She had not, but she assured me that they were headed that way. She just wanted to talk to me first. I find it interesting that teachers are like mothers. They must be all things to students. In this case, I was a diagnostician. It reminded me of the child who would not let the parents pull her very loose tooth. She wanted me to pull it for her.

Sometimes, children seem so grown up. Brad had that aura. He had dark eyes and hair. His appearance was that of a little man who knows what he wants to do. He was quite businesslike in everything. I do not remember him doing anything like a child would. He was happy in his own little world.

I was indeed most fortunate to be teaching at a time when discipline was not difficult.

Mark was almost too good. He seemed unable to relax and have fun. I used a behavior-modification system to help the students discipline themselves. Each student had a clown who represented him or her. At the end of the day, the boys and girls could put a balloon in their clown's hand if they had stayed out of trouble that day.

Mark began to loosen up and enjoy being a boy. This meant that some days he did not get a balloon for his clown.

His mother stopped by our classroom. The children were outside. She asked about Mark's clown. I told her that I considered Mark's clown on of the best on the bulletin board. I asked her to please leave things alone. She agreed to cooperate. She said he seemed happier at home.

This is not my experience, but it is worth examining. My niece told me about an incident that happened to her when she was in the first grade. She told the teacher that she had finished her work. The teacher said, "Well, find something to do." My niece answered, "But I do not have any paper." Again, the teacher told her, "Find something to do." So she took her red crayon and colored the top of her desk. The teacher was angry and made her clean her desk.

The teacher, not the student, should have cleaned the desk. It was the teacher's fault that the student had nothing to do. With first grade or any grade you should always have something ready for those who complete work quickly.

We had a supervisor who greatly believed in readiness. She declared a four-week period for readiness. We could not give our students books until we had competed this assignment. We had many fine readiness materials, and the children enjoyed doing them.

They did wonder when they would be given a book. This became so exciting. It was almost like waiting for Christmas. The time finally came. I told them that the next day we would start reading from books.

Mothers told me that their children announced, "Tomorrow we get our first book!"

It was a day of celebration. Now, we could read.

It is such a delight to see first graders realize that they really do know how to read. I will always cherish memories of having them "walk through my classroom door."

More First Graders

Chapter 3

Teaching Other Grades

My husband was a restless minister. He moved frequently. This meant that I changed positions frequently as well. My bachelor's degree qualified me to teach grades one through eight. When I applied for a new position, I was often asked, "What is you specialty?" I would reply, "What do you have open?" I usually would be hired. I did not realize it then, but this prepared me to instruct teachers in the last twelve years before my retirement. I learned the requirements for each grade level and the methods that worked both with accelerated students and those who had learning difficulties.

I taught the sixth and seventh grades most often. I taught everything but music and art. I am glad I taught when the students were mine; that is, when teachers were allowed to have control of their classrooms. This gave us the opportunity to really get to know each other. I knew the family background. I knew when an alcoholic father had stirred up trouble at home. I could give a little extra attention when a student was suffering.

We moved to Indiana so my husband could continue his education to become a Presbyterian minister. I did not think about teaching until we were settled in our new residence. My husband attended a seminary in Chicago four days a week. I was alone with my baby son, who could not converse with me. I was lonely. I decided to look for a job. I found a position at Meadow Lake School, an open country, two-classroom school. I would teach the four lower grades. At least I did not need to prepare lessons for the fifth through eighth grades.

Meadow Lake School

The two classrooms were divided by folding doors. Sometimes the school became a community center, and we pushed back the doors to make one big room. The doors did not reach the floor.

The boys in the upper grades considered this an invitation to roll marbles under the doors. They had fun until they discovered that the teacher on the other side would not return their marbles.

She just did not appreciate their clever distraction.

We had a county superintendent who would drop in unannounced. He was a fine man, quiet and businesslike. He dropped in one day when the music teacher was teaching the students a dance for a program. She was an eccentric lady who was rich enough to buy anything she wanted. She sometimes wore rundown shoes. On this particular day, she was wearing those shoes. Just as the county superintendent walked through the door, the music teacher kicked off a shoe, which flew across the room. It didn't bother her. She just laughed and picked up the shoe.

The practice stopped temporarily while the county superintendent completed his visit.

One day, the county superintendent walked in while I was teaching phonics. This was a no-no. Everything goes in cycles. At that time, phonics was taught through spelling. Teachers were not supposed to give too much attention to how the words were put together. He quietly asked if I did not think the students received enough phonics through spelling. I told him that I did not, which was why I was putting special emphasis on phonics. He smiled and said, "You go right ahead and teach the way that you think works. The important thing is not a set of rules but to give students the help they need to learn."

I stopped teaching for a year and the next time I taught I had one grade. That was in Wolcott, Indiana; I taught seventh grade and supervised the high-school study hall. I also was drafted to teach girl's PE. To me, that was the comedy of the century. I am not athletic and certainly did not want to teach a gym class. However, I was the only woman teacher who had studied physical education to complete her degree.

My husband bought books on various sports. I studied the rules and attempted to fulfill my assignment. I became the most arbitrary umpire you have ever met. If I said it was a strike then it was a strike! Exercises, however, were something I could do. It was amazing how many excuses girls found to keep from doing physical education.

Indiana winters were new to me. It was a thrill to hear the snowplows at work during the first big snow. I learned that these snowstorms can have a drastic effect on the community. The assigned bus driver would watch the snow until he decided it was time to check the bus route.

He would drive out and call back his judgment of the snow. It was not unusual for classes to be dismissed in the middle of the period. One time a busload of students were stranded out in the country near a farmhouse. The farmer and his wife fed and cared for those children until they could be rescued. The schools did not want a repeat of that situation.

There was a paved area outside one of the doors of the school. Ice would form there, and the children loved skating around on it. They were never permitted to be out very long, but it was a way for them to work off a bit of energy. They were always well supervised.

I will share another weather-related experience from this same school. It had been raining. The children had been cooped up for a few days. The sun was shining so the teachers grabbed the opportunity to take the children out for recess. Well, of course, the students got their shoes muddy. We gave the children brushes so they could clean their shoes before returning to the classroom. My class cleaned their shoes. We were just about to enter the classroom when a very irate custodian raged, "I am going to tell the principal about your students bringing mud into the school!" Sometimes I wonder if I look like a person who can be pushed around. Well, I'd had it! I turned to him and answered, "That sounds like a fantastic idea. I will go with you!"

That surprised him. He cooled down quickly and apologized for his anger. Then I told him how my students had taken extra time to be sure their shoes did not bring in mud.

Jerry's parents asked for a conference at the beginning of the school year. They told me that Jerry was a "blue baby". A blue baby has a defective heart. His face becomes pale when his heart is not performing properly. The parents had been warned that he probably would never see adulthood. They had agonized over this situation and come to terms with it. They told me that they wanted Jerry to enjoy whatever life he had. He was to run. He was to play games and be a normal child. They said I was not to worry when he turned blue. If he died while he was under my supervision, I was not to feel responsible. There were times when my heart struggled to be calm.

The blood seemed to drain from Jerry's face, which told me that his heart was not functioning properly. This happened several times through the year. I did not call the parents. I did pray a lot.

What a beautiful ending that story had! We moved, but we returned for a special event.

Jerry's parents heard that I was in town. They sent me a message telling me that Jerry had had open-heart surgery. He was doing so well that he was on the basketball team.

Marian came complaining about Fred. He didn't seem to want to hurt her, but he was pestering her. He would hit her gently and move away. She was so annoyed. She had complained to her mother about it. Her mother told her to tell me. I said, "Marian, Fred thinks you are the cutest girl he has ever seen. He is trying to get your attention. He doesn't really want to hurt you." She looked disgusted. The she replied, "You sound just like my mom. That is what she told me!" I told her that I would talk with Fred.

Students are so suspicious of notes that are sent home. Sometimes they just manage to lose them. I decided to try to remove that stigma. When a lesson was done well, I would send a note home to let the parents know about the excellent work. The results were wonderful. The student had something positive to share with the parents.

Marvin was repeating sixth grade. This meant he was taller than most of the boys in his class. He was charming. Now and then he had to test the teacher. If I looked at him, he would blush. It became a joke between us. He could not do anything without telling on himself by blushing. On Valentine's Day he gave me a blushing valentine. I treasured that card for years.

Jess couldn't resist the temptation. I had my back to the room because I was writing something on the blackboard. I heard the sound made by a piece of paper held over a comb. I did not turn around. I said, "Jess, put the comb in your pocket." Then I looked at the class. Jess's eyes were as big as dollars. He asked, "Do teachers have eyes in the back of their heads?" I laughed and answered, "Of course. How else could we cope with students like you?" Teachers should have a sense of humor.

Often a teacher receives assignments because the need is there, and she is the one the principal believes can fill the position. That was what happened to me. A high-school teacher taught my social studies class while I took charge of a troublesome high-school study hall. (I will come back to that later.) I returned to my classroom after the social studies teacher had left. There were wads of paper on the floor. I told some of the students to clean them up. Then I said. "I can tell from the position of the paper exactly who the guilty parties are." "I had better not come in again and find paper wads on the floor." The bluff paid off. There were no more paper wads.

Wolcott, Indiana

Wolcott, Indiana

Assembly, Wolcott, Indiana

I taught sixth grade at Wolcott. This is the "School News" that was printed in the town newspaper.

Sixth Grade

The sixth grade will write letters to children in foreign countries. We received our correspondents' names yesterday. Most of them came from England, but some came from Brazil, Sweden, New Zealand, Australia, Canada, Panama, Cuba, West Indies, and Hawaii.

In English, we have made a class magazine. Each pupil wrote a poem, story, riddle, or made a comic strip for his/her contribution.

Several deserve honorable mention. Catherine Arvin, Carman Collins, Marian Rauer, John Alishouse, Glenn Furrer, and Kenneth Caudle had fine stories. David Harrison, Donna Sheets, and Mary Alice Quinn had outstanding poems. Mary Quinn's covers the housing shortage, so we'll want everyone to enjoy it.

The Elves
Up in a stump lived the woodpecker boys.
They made such a lot of bothersome noise.
So the downstairs people (little Elves)
Said, "Let's find a new home for ourselves."

"Where are you going?" asked a Bee
"Why, we are moving. Can't you see?"
They stopped at a house, wee, cozy, and shady,
Where lived a mushroom Pixie Lady.
"May we board with you?"
"Oh, no indeed,
I have not more room than I need."
So they called to an old blind Mole
"We'd like a place in your tunnel hole."
No answer! They felt sad and sadder.
A young owl told them to try this ladder.
But the tower house belonged to a gnome,
Who hurried them right out of his home.
"Perhaps the ants will rent us rooms."
But they chased The Elves with tickly brooms.
Very readily, "Well its best
To ask Ground Sparrow for a nest."
"But I have only one!" she told them.
Then a toad began to scold them,
For getting in his right of way,
"But we must find a home today,"
Said a little old man mouse"
"I know a quiet empty house."
"I'll take a toe." It was a shoe
They moved right in (and the mouse did too).

Mary Alice Quinn

I told you that I would come back to my experience supervising a troublesome high-school study hall in Wolcott. At that time, we lived in Remington, Indiana, another farming community located nearby. Both communities were known for their wonderful corn, tomatoes, and chickens.

Anytime there was trouble anywhere nearby you heard about it. The rumor was that a high-school teacher, a young man, was having a difficult time. It was rumored that the boys were teasing the teacher by tossing his shoes around the room.

I had not the faintest idea that this would affect me. That is, until I received my schedule for the last semester. There it was! I would be supervising the troublesome study hall. That was why the high-school teacher was teaching my social studies class.

I was still young and smaller than some of the students. The bell rang for classes to begin. I watched as the high-school students came to the room.

As soon as the students were seated, three boys stood up. They looked at me.

I asked, "Are you going to the restroom?"

One of them answered, "Yes, we thought we would."

I did not flinch. I replied, "Well, my work assignment said that I would be supervising a high-school study hall. Now, if you all need to go to the restroom, I will line you up and take you."

The leader smiled. He said, "We do not really need to go to the restroom."

"I thought that was probably true," I answered. "So take your seats, and let's get to work."

They did. As always, I was a roving teacher. I walked up and down the rows, stopping occasionally to look at work. The students liked this. Sometimes I could help with their work.

Later in the year, the coach sent me two redheads. I asked, "Why are you here?" One of them replied, "We went to sleep in class." I smiled and said, "Don't let me disturb your nap. Put your heads down and sleep." Of course they could not sleep, but they did keep their heads down.

They were with me for several days. The coach said they could return to class. We had had a great time while they were with me.

My experience as supervisor of that high-school study hall can only be classified as wonderful. What fine students they were!

I taught in two schools where a minority group was prominent. One school was 60 percent black. My hair had begun to turn gray, so I was obviously older than many of the teachers. The students decided to put me to the test. They were arrogant and disobedient. I loved teaching, but I did not like being a policewoman. This was required in this position. I became ill, but I refused to be driven from my teaching position. One afternoon as I left the school I said, "Lord, I asked you for a place to serve. If this is where you want me, you must strengthen me and give me courage to face each day!" I will tell you how he answered that prayer a bit later.

I did not have many absences due to illness. I wanted to be present. My students were important to me. I knew them and their needs. I felt that I could do a better job than a substitute teacher. One day, however, I did not have a choice.

It was a time when integration was just beginning. The students weren't quite sure how to deal with a white teacher, even though I am part Choctaw Indian. Their philosophy seemed to be, "If I can get away with anything, it is all right." The problem arose if they got caught. Knowing this, I tried to keep temptation out of the way. I put my purse and anything else I did not want bothered in a locked cabinet.

One day, I was ill, and the class was to have a substitute teacher. I sent her the key to the cabinet and suggested that it would be wise for her to lock her purse inside. The substitute was young and naïve. She thought I was being an "old fogey." She not only left her purse on the desk, she left it open. Later, she was devastated when someone took her billfold.

The principal called me and asked if I had any idea who would do such a thing. I told him that it might be anyone in the sixth-hour class. I told him I would deal with it when I returned. Frankly, I thought the substitute had it coming. She should not have tempted the students.

I returned to school the next day. Several students met me as I entered the door. One of them asked, "Did you know that someone took that teacher's billfold!" I told them that I had heard about the incident, but I did not discuss it with them. During the last hour of class, everyone was seated. Tension filled the room, I knew I had to deal with the problem. I stepped in front of my desk and looked at them.

"You know what happened yesterday," I said. "I look at you, and I don't want to think that any of you took the billfold. I also know that the billfold did not get out of the purse without help. Sometimes we do foolish things that can ruin our reputations. Now, I would like to make a bargain with you. If the person who took the billfold returns it with all of its contents, I will never tell anyone who did this terrible deed. Does that seem fair to you?"

They agreed. Everyone began the assignment.

As always, I was a roving teacher. I moved up and down the aisles. I saw a hand reach out. I took a note and walked to my desk. I read, "I took the billfold. It is in my locker with everything in it." I wrote her a note asking if she needed to go to the restroom. She held up her hand. I went to her and gave her the hallway pass. She hurried from the room. I had a newspaper on my desk. I picked it up and carried it as I continued moving around the room. When I saw the girl coming, I stepped out and took the billfold, covering it with the paper. I hurried to the principal's office and placed the paper and billfold on his desk. My other students didn't miss me.

The principal was talking on the telephone when I walked into his office. I left the school before he could talk with me. He called my home and wanted to know who had taken the billfold. I told him about my bargain with the students. He tried to force the answer from me, but I never told him.

I have often thought about that incident. The guilty person was the last one I would have suspected. No one talked about it after that day.

Students often develop behavioral problems when they are behind in their classwork. This is probably a way to cope with a deficiency. Wesley was such a student. He was supposed to be in the sixth grade. He could read, but the effort was more than he wanted to give. Out of curiosity, I asked him to read to me. He had a severe tracking problem. His eyes would wander down the page as he was attempting to read. Reading made no sense to him, so he did not enjoy it. It seemed that the effort just wasn't worth the results. Instead, he would try to cause a distraction in the classroom. He was already far behind. What does a teacher do in such a case? Sometimes I would ask the parents to tutor. Many of them were willing, but they could not work with their children. Wesley's parents and I did the best we could, but I was not happy with his progress. I needed to tutor him on an individual basis and that could have made a difference. I think about Wesley. What happened to him? Was he one of the many who fall by the wayside and get into trouble? I hope not.

Several students had chips on their shoulders. Most of the students I taught worked well with me. I was expected to take my turn supervising the hallways at noon. I am a strong believer in a very real God. He has walked with me throughout my life. One of my students became my special angel. He was head and shoulders taller than I am. He seemed always to be present when trouble brewed. I can remember two times when he rescued me.

I had been given specific instructions to keep the gymnasium door closed during the lunch period. One day, a rather large student opened the door. I told him we were not supposed to open the gym door at noon. He sneered and opened the door wider. I started toward him. My angel moved ahead of me. He said, "You heard the lady. Close the door!" The rebellious student closed the door, and there was no more trouble.

It was noon, and the students were milling around the school entrance. One girl intentionally brushed against me. Then she turned and looked angrily at me. She started to say something. My angel stepped between us. He put his arm around her shoulders and moved her away. He talked with her. She never bothered me again.

One final story about my angel: The University of Central Oklahoma asked me to fill in during a faculty member's sabbatical. This was the answer to the prayer I'd made during a moment of complete frustration over having to police rather than teach. I returned to the school to pick up my belongings. I came during class time, so I did not expect to see my special angel.

I was walking down the hall when I felt his arm around my shoulders. And there he was. He asked, "Why did you leave us? We need you so." That was heartbreaking, but I needed to accept this golden opportunity. My health was being destroyed by the constant policing that had become necessary at that school. The next year there was a vacancy in the reading department.

I became a fulltime faculty member. I immediately started classes toward my doctorate.

My seventh-grade class had been to the library. As far as I knew, everything was fine. Then one of the boys began raging and became quite unruly. I asked him to quiet down. He ignored my request. I walked back to where he was and asked him again for order. He continued to misbehave. Suddenly, I reached out and pinned him against the lockers.

He said, "Get you hands off of me! Ain't nobody touches me!"

I looked him right in the eyes. I said, "Well, I am! You straighten up and behave yourself. If you don't I will march you to the principal's office and paddle you. I will do the paddling. I am angry! Do you want that?"

He meekly replied, "No, Ma'am."

I asked, "Can you act like a man and do what you know you should do?"

He said, "Yes, Ma'am."

The custodian saw the entire episode. As the students marched toward the classroom, I said, "Mean old woman!" The custodian replied, "Mean old woman nothing. You should have put him in the locker and locked it."

The incident had a very interesting outcome. This student bragged that someone liked him. He told the other students that he knew who cared about him. He told them that he knew who would always help him. This even carried over into the next grade level.

I explained to the students, "I do not give grades. You make grades. I will do everything I can to help you understand what is expected of you. I will see that you know how to proceed. Your grade will be based on your performance. Good work deserves good grades.

A fine and intelligent student did really well during the first grading period. Then he became lazy. His sloppy work received a C. Later he said, "You know, Mrs. Poe, I was really angry at you for giving me a C."

I answered, "I didn't give you a C."

He smiled. "I know. I made a C." Now we could talk.

"Right," I said. "I also noticed that you decided to do something about that C." His work improved. I am almost certain he made an A in the course.

What a joy it is when the student takes responsibility for doing well in class! I was always willing to go the extra mile for my students. I was not there to fail them. I was there to teach them.

The assignment was, "How to write a friendly letter." I wanted to try something new, so I wrote a friendly letter to my students. I used my letter to explain the procedure for writing a friendly letter. I told them they could write about anything they liked. Wow! I was completely unprepared for what happened. The students knew their letters would not be shared with the class, so they poured out their hearts. These students had more problems than you can imagine. Some of them told me about boy/girl troubles. Others told me about troubles with parents and home in general. I became an "Ann Landers." This meant that we wrote more than one friendly letter. I furnished the envelopes and paper. I did a lot of counseling through those letters. I remained true to my promise; I did not reveal any of the subject matter covered in our letter exchanges. The assignment lasted a bit longer than I had intended, but I guess that was all right, too.

Our classrooms surrounded an open mall. The students could not get into the open area, but they could enjoy the plants. One evening I was a bit late leaving my room. I had placed my purse on top of my desk and was ready to leave. The other teachers were gone. My door opened and in walked a high-school boy. He said, "I would like to borrow a quarter." I knew I was at a disadvantage, but I looked straight at him and said, "I do not make a habit of loaning money to students. If I loan you a quarter, when will you pay me back?" He grinned and said, "Oh, I will pay you back tomorrow." I gave him the quarter and he left, as did I as quickly as I could.

The next day I saw this student. I asked him for my quarter. He looked so smug and said, "I don't have a quarter." He walked off. Later that same day, he was bouncing a basketball in the hall. I got the ball. He came up to me and said. "I want the ball." I replied, "I want my quarter." He grinned and reached into his pocket. He returned my quarter. I told him that it was against the rules to play with the ball in the halls. I gave the ball to him but assured him that the next time I would keep the ball. He did not break the rules again. And I did not dilly-dally around after school again.

I had grown up in a rural area of southeastern Oklahoma. I had not been around black people. I do not believe that I am prejudiced against them or any other group of people. I am prejudiced, however, against an attitude that I saw in black students. I believe many of them sell themselves short. They are very capable and can succeed in most anything they wish. I see no reason for crying that the world is against them because they are black.

I am seven-sixteenths Choctaw Indian. I have experienced people's prejudice. I know what it feels like to have someone think he is better because he has a lighter skin than I do. That has not kept me from proving my worth. I am a stubborn person. I dug in my heels and said, "I will show you that I can succeed!" And I did.

The only other ethnic group I taught was in a Plains Indian Boarding School. Foolish me; I thought I would be accepted by all American Indians. That did not prove to be true. I was from the wrong tribe.

The students readily accepted me. The teachers were another matter.

CONCHO INDIAN SCHOOL

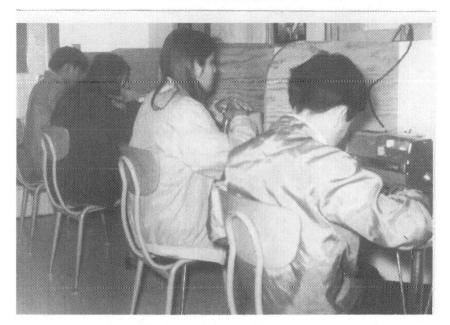

Concho Indian School

The superintendent permitted a doctoral student to test all of our students over the intercom. Teachers would remain in the classrooms, but we could not explain the test to the students or answer any questions about it. I believe the doctoral student's theory was that American Indians were falling below the standard for school performance. My students were frustrated, and so was their teacher.

At the end of the semester, I gave the students a different version of the same test. First, I explained the importance of doing their best on the test. I told them about permanent records and how these records would follow them throughout life. One fine-looking student raised his hand to ask a question. He asked, "Is that true?" When I assured him that it was, he muttered, "Oh, my goodness. I was so angry at that lady who gave us the tests at the beginning of the year, I just put down anything." I told him this was his opportunity to show what his skills really were.

The entire class benefited from the discussion. They did well on the end-of-the-year test.

There was really no way to compare the two tests.

Expectations are so important. I wanted to decorate a rather large bulletin board. The other teachers told me that I would be sorry. The students would tear it up, they said. The principal told me to give it a try. I put up a three-dimensional crepe paper Christmas tree, complete with glass ornaments and gifts underneath. The students watched. I asked, "Would you like to help put up this bulletin board?" It was surprising to see how much enthusiasm they showed. Together, we put up a gorgeous Christmas bulletin board. Did they tear it up? No, they did stand in front of it, enjoying it. After Christmas, they helped me take it down.

These students lived in dormitories. One morning, the girls appeared in Indian headdresses they had made the evening before. I thought they were fabulous. The principal came to me during the last period and said, "Well, I have not heard from you."

"About what?" I asked.

"The headdresses," she said.

"Weren't they great!" I replied. "I wish they had made one for me."

She smiled. "That is how I felt, too." Apparently, she'd had many complaints about the girls' works of art.

Ben was hostile in class. He wouldn't cooperate, which was so out of character for him. I asked him to see me after my last class. "Something is bothering you," I said. "Let's talk about it. You should not keep hidden whatever is not sitting well with you." He seemed so surprised. He asked, "Why do you think something is wrong?" I reminded him that he had been rude and did not want to cooperate in class. He was astounded that I'd noticed. "Yes, I do have a problem," he admitted. "But I did not realize I was bringing it into the classroom. The trouble is in the dormitory." I encouraged him to talk about it. I told him that I had no jurisdiction over what went on in the dormitory, but that I could listen and that might help. He appreciated my concern and told me that he would be more careful about his attitude. He held true to his word.

I like to set boundaries the first day of school. The grade doesn't matter. Students like to know what is expected of them. At the Indian Boarding School, I told the students that my desk was my territory, and they were not to invade that property. I also told them that their desks were their territory, and I would never search their desks without a reason and unless they were present.

The school furnished materials for the teachers. We submitted our needs to the principal and these things were issued to us. The students thought it was a great sport to sneak pencils from the teacher's desk. One day, I said, "Oh, I guess it is time that I requisitioned more pencils."

A student said, "Do you want pencils? I can get some for you." I said, "No, I do not think you should do that. That is wrong."

She tossed her head and asked, "What difference does it make? It is just the government anyway."

"Who or what is the government?" I asked.

She answered, "Oh, it's those people in Washington."

"No, you are mistaken," I answered. " You are the government. You, your parents, and your friends, we are the government. Those people in Washington represent us."

The students all started asking questions. We had a lively discussion. They now had a better understanding of the part they played in "the government."

Teaching at this school was one of the most difficult positions I had in my thirty-four years of teaching. First, I was from the wrong tribe. Choctaws are from the five civilized tribes. These tribes were more settled in one area with a governing body. The Plains Tribes were hunters and moved around. Second, I came to the school as part of a program funded by Title I. Third, I was not in the teacher's union.

The teachers worked with me only when they could do nothing else. Otherwise, they shunned me. Now, if you have never been shunned, you cannot imagine what it is like. One of teachers was an art teacher who was to meet me under different circumstances later in my life. I considered her work to be quite good.

One of the first things I realized at the school was that the students sort of drifted into class when they pleased. I told them that the class started at eight o'clock and that I expected them to be in their seats, ready for work, at that time. A girl shyly said, "Oh, we come to class on 'Indian time.'"

I looked directly at the class and replied, "You will be living and working in the white man's world. It is my job to teach you how to live and work in that world. I can guarantee you that you will not hold a job by coming whenever it pleases you. Now, I do not intend to fuss at you. I will have a list of students on my desk. I will put your class arrival time on that record. One day we will have a day of reckoning." With that, we began our work.

I did exactly what I had told them. Most of the students arrived on time. One day, I called out the names of the students who had been late and told them to be in the room at four o'clock. When they arrived, I had cleaning materials ready. I made the stragglers clean the room thoroughly. Then I thanked and dismissed them. Later the room needed a little extra cleaning. I said, "I wish some of you would be late again. The room needs cleaning." One of the students said, "No way! I don't want to clean the room anymore." We all had a good laugh. They had learned their lesson.

Working under government requirements was new to me. One day, I wanted a light bulb unscrewed; it was causing a glare on the screen. I went to the office and asked, "Could someone unscrew the light bulb right in front of the film screen?" The secretary said, "You will need a work order on that." A work order was required for what I would have done myself if I'd had a ladder. I could not believe it. Yes, I could see the reasoning behind it—the government has to keep track of projects and materials—but I had always done much of what needed to be done without asking anyone's permission.

I taught seventh-grade reading for several years.   One school hired me specifically for that purpose but had me teach history until funding arrived for the reading program. When the money arrived, I was moved to a room next to the principal's office. It had to be the dirtiest room I had ever seen, so I started coming early with cleaning materials in hand. One morning, I emptied the shelves of their books and pulled the bookcases from the wall. I was just started to   sweep the dirt from behind a bookcase when I hear the principal say, "Mrs. Poe, didn't anyone tell you that it is against the rules to sweep behind the bookcases?" He had a big smile on his face. He said, "You do not have to do that. I will send the janitor."

The janitor arrived and did the job graciously. The next morning I was on a chair trying to dust the film screen when the janitor said, "I will be glad to do that. I just did not know you wanted it done." There had to have been an inch of dirt on that screen.

This school was a most delightful experience. The students were so excited about learning new methods of reading. They especially enjoyed studying vocabulary. We learned a new word and found synonyms and antonyms for it. We developed our own vocabulary book.

Piner Middle School, Sherman, Texas

Controlled Readers were used to increase speed and comprehension. We had stories with comprehension questions for several levels of learning. The student could choose more difficult films as comprehension scores improved.

Students gained an appreciation for new books. Sometimes we would break into groups and have a lively discussion focused on a book they had read.

Discipline was never a problem. They enjoyed coming to class. The work was mostly individualized. Each student had a folder with assignments for the day. The student picked up his/her folder when he/she arrived.

At a school in Claremore, Oklahoma, I was presented an empty room and a sum of money. I was to determine the kind of furniture, books, and other equipment I might need for that room. Wow!

What an assignment! I would see all seventh graders at some time during the day. It was my job to teach them reading skills.

I presented my list of books and equipment to the principal. He looked at me and said, "You do know, don't you, that you are teaching seventh grade?"

"Oh, yes, sir, I'll bet you do not know that the learning range in my seventh grade will be from first grade to the college level?"

He replied, "Well, you seem to know what you are doing. Go ahead with your plans."

As he looked over the list of materials, he remarked, "Mrs. Smith has a set of these books stored away in her cabinet. She didn't know how to use them. That will save you some money."

It was surprising how many items the school already had stored away. The principal was so interested in this new thing that was starting in his school. I invited him to visit anytime and see for himself the wide range of reading ability in any classroom. It would be more evident in my reading class.

I would take a group to practice some special skill. Reader's Digest published readers at several levels. Some of them were at a first grade level, but the stories were for older students.

I purchased the entire set. Reader's Digest offered a gift with large purchases. I chose classical music recordings. Often, when the students were working and everything was quiet, I would play the music softly.

At first, the students grumbled. They begged to be allowed to bring their music from home. I told them the music was also a learning experience. They learned to appreciate the classical music. Sometimes, one of them would enter the room saying, "Play a selection from Bach or Beethoven."

Teachers always appreciate a greeting like this: "It is so much fun coming to this class."

"Why is that?" I asked.

"Well, we never know what we are going to do until we get here. Then, whatever it is, we like doing the work."

I had two tape recorders. These were for oral reading. When we studied poetry, I told the students to choose their favorite poem and read it aloud. They were to read it over and over until they were pleased with their presentation. I would critique that reading. It was surprising how many boys read Edgar Allan Poe's "Annabelle Lee."

Oh, yes, we had tests. I laugh when I remember one essay test. Elizabeth was such a bright student. That was why checking her test was so amusing. Obviously she did not have a clue about the answer, but she decided to "test" the teacher. She wrote and wrote, but nothing remotely pertained to the question. I wrote at the top of her test, Nice try, Elizabeth.

I remember another essay test. I turned the page, and there at the top was a note: "Same old test."

Suzanne loved reading. She excelled in all of the lessons. She came to me and asked if she might be excused from reading with the controlled reader. I asked why she wished to be removed from that requirement. She explained, "It slows me down." So she did not read on the machine anymore.

We had a State Spelling Bee. Suzanne was our state winner. She was also second runner up in the National Spelling Bee. A reporter asked her how she had learned spelling so well.

She answered, "I read a lot."

Her father was simply astounded that his daughter could out-read him. He asked if the school offered reading lessons for adults. We had those lessons during the summer. He was a lawyer. This meant that he needed to carefully examine his reading information. He could not relax and read, so Suzanne could our-read him.

One day, I looked up to see the principal strolling around the room, observing what the students were doing. He spent a good part of the hour moving from one area to the other. Later, he told me that I was correct when I said that a wide range of learning skills would be present in this class.

Comments like the principal's remark—"You do know, don't you, that you are teaching seventh grade?"—are taken for granted far too often. I once heard a third-grade teacher say, "I am teaching third grade. Everyone will read at the third-grade level!" In truth, that would be a rare class. All teachers should remember that there is always a range of learning skills in any grade.

I wince when our presidents promise that every child will learn to read. There are so many factors involved in whether a child learns to read, especially at his or her grade level.

My son and daughter could read before they entered school. That was partly because we spent time reading with and to them. When my son was in the third grade, the librarian in our town would not allow children to check out books that were not at their grade level. Then a new librarian took over. She visited the schools and told the children they could check out anything they wished. I shall never forget the excitement this created. My son and several of his friends dashed into our house announcing this, chattering about the books they wanted. Well, of course, some of the books they brought back were too advanced for them. They soon found this out and returned to the library for books they could read. At least they did not feel locked in to one level.

Every teacher should have the privilege of teaching one class filled with accelerated students. They were not chosen for that class simply because they were bright and eager to learn; that was just a happenstance. What a challenge and a joy they were.

The first day, I explained that we would begin with no rules. We would make the rules as they were needed. For example, if students sharpened pencils too often, a limit would be set. We did quite well without rules. Of course, some rules became necessary.

Jeff was so attracted to Nancy. He foolishly grabbed her carefully written theme and wadded it up. She was crushed. We had to do something, so I asked the class for suggestions. How should Jeff be punished? A hand shot up. "Yes," I asked. "What do you suggest?"

Tom said, "You should paddle him!"

"Well, I could do that, but let's take a look at that suggestion. It would give me some exercise, but it would not do anything to correct the wrong."

Another hand went up. "Yes, Vera, what do you suggest?"

"He should copy Nancy's theme until she is happy with it." The class agreed. Jeff had Nancy's attention.

The principal wanted a teacher to attend the PTA planning meeting. He asked me to do this. I resisted because my accelerated class was in session. He assured me that he would take care of the class. I told the students where I would be and why. The meeting lasted longer than expected. I was worried about my class. The principal went to my room. He assured me that everyone was busy. He said the students were working so hard, they did not even know he was there.

We had many outside activities. We went on a trip to Oklahoma City, where we attended the legislature while it was in session. One of our students was chosen as a page for that session. Woodward is located in the far western part of the state and some of the students had not been to Oklahoma City.

We wanted to make the most of our visit. We brought a picnic lunch that we decided to eat at Lincoln Park Zoo. This way we could enjoy the beautiful outdoors and the animals.

We made other trips. These were possible because the students had already completed the lessons required for the year. Most of the students were on the honor roll when they started junior high. Someone complimented me on my good work with the students. I explained that these students just needed the opportunity to learn. They were ready and eager to move ahead in everything. I have always felt that they were a rare blessing, a gift to me.

Still, some students enjoyed testing the teacher. One year, a sixth-grade boy took advantage of a pile of papers on my desk. He placed a toy mouse under the papers. The whole class knew he had done this. They all waited expectantly. I sensed something was amiss. I saw the mouse tail as I approached the desk. I looked at the class. Then I reached over and pulled the mouse from under the papers. I asked, "Toby, does this belong to you?" He nodded as I handed the mouse to him. The class laughed, but not at me. The joke was over.

The coat closet was at the back of the classroom. One Friday, the students retrieved their coats and hats as they left for the day. On Monday, Tim came to me. It seems that someone had taken his brother Joe's cap from the cloakroom on Friday. Tim and Joe had been in town on Saturday and saw a small boy wearing the cap; the boy was with their classmate Max. Their natural reaction was to take it away from the child, but their very wise mother suggested that they bring the problem to the school. That was where the trouble had begun. Tim came to me with the story. I went to the principal and asked, "What should I do?" This was a time when sensible paddling was permitted. The principal said that I should paddle Max, but first I must get a confession.

I took Max to the principal's office, but we had to wait for the principal to complete a telephone call. We stood there in the hall waiting. I did not say anything to Max or explain why we were there. When we walked into the principal's office, I asked, "Max, why did you take the cap?" Big tears filled his eyes, and he answered, "My brother needs a cap." I told him that stealing was the wrong way to provide his brother with a cap. I explained that it was not my desire to paddle him, but the principal and I wanted him to remember never to steal again. I swatted him a couple of times. Did this solve the problem? I do not remember what happened, but I suspect someone in that fine town helped the family in need.

In all of the years that I taught, I do not remember ever sending students to the principal for punishment. I took care of the discipline myself.

Marvin, a seventh-grader, was sent to the principal's office by the music teacher. I was called to the principal's office because Marvin was my student. It was easy to see that Marvin had been crying. I turned to the principal and asked, "Why is Marvin here? What has he done?" The principal was hesitant in his answer. I said, "Do you mean to tell me that Marvin has been punished, but you do not know why?" It seems that the music teacher thought Marvin was singing off-key. I turned to Marvin and said, "Why don't you go to our room? Things will be all right."

Some teachers like to tell their colleagues how they should be teaching. I always felt that was not my place. A first-year teacher was in the room next to mine. We marched our students to lunch and other activities. She always started ahead of me. She gave instructions as they stood in line. She was so frustrated because her students moved around and were restless.

One day she came to my room. She said, "Now, you know what I am doing wrong. Why don't you tell me?" I told her that I did not make a practice of telling other teachers what they should do. "Since you asked I will tell you. Give your instructions while your students are seated. When you get them on their feet, march them."

"Of course," she responded. She thanked me and followed my instructions.

Woodward experienced a terrible destruction in 1947. Three tornadoes went through the downtown area. One hundred six people died. My class was studying transportation. Woodward had a small airport, but it was not for commercial use. When I asked if anyone had ridden in a large airplane, two boys looked at each other and grinned. I asked, "Well, have you ridden a large airplane?" Jimmy answered, "Yes, we have, but we knew nothing about the ride. We were flown to Oklahoma City for medical attention following the tornado.

The boys each had large scars across the back of their heads.

When this story surfaced, other students wanted to talk about the tornado. Dan told about the mother cat that removed her kittens from their house. He said she kept crying until the door was opened. She left and was gone for a long time. She came back and proceeded to move all of the kittens. The sky was blue, and there was no evidence that such horror would come to the Woodward area. Dan's home was destroyed in the tornado. How did the cat know that was going to happen?

It was my turn to be on duty at recess. We had hardly gotten outside when I noticed a huge very dark cloud forming in the southwest. Woodward had already experienced a severe tornado. I didn't know what that black cloud moving toward us meant, but I did know that it could not be good. I ran into the building and rang the bell to end recess. By this time the children had spotted the ugly cloud headed our way. They dashed for the door and safety. We had barely gotten in when the wind hit. It grabbed the door we had just passed through and tore it from its hinges.

I was the head teacher in this building. The telephone was ringing. I hurried to answer it. It was the principal calling from another school. He said, "Tell the teachers it is not a tornado, but it is a strong, straight wind. Everything will be all right."

I first told my class and quickly began conveying the principal's message to the rest of the teachers. I approached one room and could hear the voices saying, "The Lord is my shepherd." This touched me so that I could hardly open the door to give them the message. When I did, the teacher told me that reciting the psalm had been a student's request.

I do not believe that we lived in fear, but we did have a deep respect for the fierce storms that came our way. We practiced safety rules for dealing with these times.

Woodward is in the plains area of northwestern Oklahoma, where sandstorms occur now and then. We were studying soil conservation just before one of these sandstorms hit. A student noticed that the soil flying past our windows was black. He remarked, "Well, there goes Colorado." Our sand was red.

Many interesting things happened in my seven years with the Woodward public schools One of the experiences involved visiting our students' homes. I made an appointment with a parent, and a mother would take my class while I made this call. I remember going to Darrell's home. His wonderful mother had the house shining and greeted me warmly. We were having a good visit, but she seemed uncomfortable. Finally, she blurted our, "Well, when are you going to tell me?"

"Tell you what?" I asked.

"About Darrell's temper," she said.

"What about Darrell's temper? I have not experienced his temper."

"Well, he has one. He certainly exhibits it at home!"

I assured her that he was a well-behaved, good student at school. She breathed easier then. I did wonder what happened at that home after my visit.

I was teaching at the University of Central Oklahoma when the teachers received an invitation to a sale at a Sight and Sound store. Our daughter had expressed a desire for a music system. Sight and Sound had some interesting ones on sale. My husband and I decided to check out the sale, which was in south Oklahoma City. We walked through the door and were greeted by a handsome young man. He smiled and said, "You must be Mrs. Poe."

I answered, "Yes, I am. Do I know you?"

His smile grew bigger as he replied, "Well, you should."

So, I asked, "Do I teach one of your children?"

He kept grinning. "Oh, no, Ma'am. You taught me."

I told him that he would need to help me. "Where did I teach you?"

He smiled and answered, "Woodward, Oklahoma." And then he told me his name. I asked, "Did you and Billy ever quit fighting?" Then he really laughed. He explained, "We are and were good friends, but we did like to fight. We didn't really want to hurt each other."

Supervision of the restroom was important. I used the monitor system. One day, another teacher was standing with me as we waited for the students to complete their restroom visits. She asked me who was my monitor for the boy's restroom. When I told her Jim was in charge, she said, "Don't you know that you can't trust him? He comes from a rough family." Just then, Jim came out of the restroom and announced that everything had gone well. I was so proud that I could say, "Thank you, Jim, for doing your work well. Enjoy your recess." It really angered me to see a child branded because someone else in his family might have done something wrong.

Jim never gave me reason to expect anything but the best where he was concerned.

Teachers are sometimes called on to do unusual things. Once, I was called to the telephone. A very distraught mother said, "My former husband is in town from California. I have been told that he has plans to kidnap our daughters and take them away. Please won't you hide them where he cannot find them! I will come for them as soon as I can."

I related this message to the principal. He told me to send the girls to him. I told the girls about their mother's call. The girls readily agreed to comply with their mother's request. I was afraid they might object, but they did not seem to want to see their father.

The principal hid them in the dining area. Then he asked me to see if I could find them. I could not. The girls did their work in their hiding place. Everything worked out well.

Today, I watched the first snowfall of the winter. The flakes floated and turned with the wind. It is always a thrill to see the very first snow. It brought to mind a seventh-grade reading class in Claremore, Oklahoma. It was March 11, but there was snow. The students kept glancing at the drifting snow. I said, "Why don't we all go to the windows and enjoy the snow?" They were delighted. We had talked as we watched, but they soon became bored. Now we could work without distraction.

That night, ice covered the trees and electric wires. Wires were broken, and there was no electricity. School was cancelled the next day. We returned to school two days later. Again, here came the snow. The students' reaction was quite different. Someone said, "Oh, no!" The snow had lost its beauty and had become a problem.

Sixth-grade students are so enthusiastic about learning new things. Science lends itself to these kinds of projects. We were studying reptiles. One of my students was a friend of the zoo's herpetology manager, who loaned us a nonpoisonous snake to study. We kept it in a glass cage located near the pencil sharpener. Naturally, all of the students had pencils that needed sharpening. Our snake would strike at the side of the cage when anyone was near. I felt so sorry for the snake. His head must have been terribly sore.

Teachers from several schools met in my room that evening. The snake was still hostile. The next morning the snake was calm, but it had shed its skin. I asked the students, "Do you suppose the change in the snake's behavior has anything to do with the changing of the skin?"

The students raced for the encyclopedia and other science books. Sure enough! A snakes eyes cloud over just before it sheds its skin. That was why the snake seemed so hostile the day before.

Another science project involved "simple machines." We had a long table at the back of the room. I introduced the lesson and challenged the students to make or bring examples of simple machines. I was astounded at the response. The table was full of levers, things making use of pulleys, wedges, inclined planes, wheels and axles and screws.

It was always interesting to divide the class into groups and give each group a question to study. These discussion groups were told to keep the noise at a minimum. But sometimes they would become excited and enthusiastic about what they were studying. One day, our door opened, and the principal came in. "Are we making too much noise?" I asked. "Oh, no," he said. "I want to be part of whatever is going on in here." The students kept on with the work they had underway. The principal moved from one group to the other, listening and occasionally making a suggestion. When I called time and pulled the class back together, the principal stayed to hear the findings of each group. He thanked us for letting him be involved.

Have you ever heard your students evaluate your teaching? I once overheard two sixth-grade boys discussing me. One of them said, "Gosh, she's hard." The other one replied, "Yes, she is, but she is fair." What better evaluation could you want?

What does a teacher do when tragedy strikes one of her students? Phillip seemed perfectly healthy. No one was prepared for him to die from polio. No one knew that he was ill when he left school that afternoon. We got the report that he was ill the next day. The principal told us Phillip was in the hospital. Before the day was over, Phillip was dead. We were all stunned.

Counselors were not so prevalent at that time, so in class we talked about polio and the terrible things it did to people. Some students cried. We all grieved. We also talked about ways we could protect ourselves from catching diseases.

John was the principal's son. He thought this gave him special privileges. I could never figure out where that thought originated. It certainly did not start with me. I resented John's attitude. We were writing letters to students overseas. I walked by his desk to see what he was writing. His letter said, "My father is the principal. This gives me special privileges, I think."

"Shame on you," I said. "You are too smart to need to lean on your father's name. If I were you, I would not want someone to think that is how I got good grades or any other privileges. I believe I would tear that letter up and start over. You have enough interesting things to talk about besides your smugness." As I left his desk, he was tearing up his letter. He did write a very good letter.

John also told me that I was not teaching math correctly. This was the sixth grade, and only the simplest form of this particular math problem was introduced. He had proudly told the class that his father, the principal, had said that I was not teaching this concept correctly. I was just starting the math class when the door opened and in walked the principal. I welcomed him and said, "I am so glad that you are here. You can show the class the correct way to teach the math."

"No," he replied. "I came to apologize for what I told John about the way you are presenting this concept. You are presenting the concept appropriately for the sixth grade. I should not have made that comment to John."

Karen had very poor eyesight. She had to sit very close to the blackboard to read it. The students' eyes were tested. He eyes showed a decided need for glasses. I called her parents. Her father came to the school and listened to the report. I knew these people did not have money, but I could have referred them to the local Lion' Club, which would have been glad to help. Buying glasses where they are needed and the money is not available is their special project. Her father dismissed the problem by saying, "All she needs to do is eat more carrots."

Chapter 4

Student Stories

This year I would be teaching third grade. We were just getting acquainted when the principal visited our room. She asked to speak with me. I followed her out of the room. She said we had a problem. There were too many fifth and sixth graders. She wanted someone to take a split class load. I told her I would be glad to do that. I grouped my students anyway. She would need to find a way to keep my third graders happy while she moved them to another teacher.

She explained the situation to my third grade. The move was going well. Almost all of the students had bid me farewell and moved toward their new room. Virginia just could not take it. She looked up at me and burst into tears. That was a rough moment for me. I wanted to join her.

Instead of third grade I would have a combination class of fifth and sixth grade. We would have a most interesting year together. This was the year that Individualized Reading came into being. I loved it. It took some work but it was fun for both the student and me. I made a flyer explaining what the class would do. We were asked to exhibit our new method for the State Teacher's Meeting in Oklahoma City.

Our school had a no nonsense consultant who watched everything that the school did.

When the principal asked us to do the exhibit for the State Teachers Meeting, I agreed on condition that Mrs. Consultant would work with us. This meant that we saw her often. Many of the younger teachers dreaded seeing her enter their door. That was not so with my class. They greeted her warmly. We listened to her suggestions, but we added ours also. The

Daily Oklahoman even took our picture and printed an article about us. My students became so spoiled, they thought any special person coming to our school just had to be coming to see us.

We had a bulletin board for any creative work the students did well. Ann was staying in the room during recess. She may have returned from having been ill. I was looking at this bulletin board. I said, "I wish someone would write a poem for our bulletin board." She brightened up and asked, "You want a poem?" When I assured her that I did, she started writing. We had a special basket for contributions for this special bulletin board. She not only wrote one poem, she wrote many. I encouraged her to illustrate the poems. She gladly did so. She made a book of poems.

We sent a copy of her book of poems to Bennett Cerf's Publishing Company. She received a very nice letter from Bennett Cerf's wife, who was an Oklahoman. She encouraged Ann to keep writing.

Remember our consultant. She stopped by the bulletin board and said, "You should not be exhibiting this poem. It has a misspelled word in it." I replied, "Yes, it does. You are missing the point. I want Ann to express herself freely. I can teach her spelling on something else." She never criticized our work again.

Ann's poems were the door to learning for her. She had been a dreamer. She became enthusiastic about learning. The entire class enjoyed her work. Unfortunately the next teacher did not. She put a stop to all of that nonsense.

It was spring! Julie brought me a beautiful bouquet. Mark was standing nearby while I thanked Julie for the flowers. He said, "I was bringing you some flowers this morning." "What happened?" I asked. He hung his head and answered, "Golly gee, Mrs. Poe! How do you think I looked walking down the sidewalk carrying a bouquet of flowers?"

Mark's mother was responsible for my being "Teacher of the Day." A radio station did this special treat for some teacher each day. The teacher had to be nominated by her/his class.

Mark and his mother got the class to write a letter to the radio station. The teacher would receive a beautiful orchid.

That morning as I arrived at school a teacher greeted me with, "Well, aren't you something!" I replied, "I don't know. What are you talking about?" "Oh, didn't you know that you are the teacher of the day?" I told her that I seldom listened to the radio. She said, "Well, look surprised when your gift is delivered to you."

Our room faced the street. My students were so excited when the florist delivery van stopped at the front door. Then the knock on our door was almost more than they could stand.

They clapped as the deliveryman handed me the orchid. I wore the orchid all day. PTA met that night so I even showed the orchid off for them.

The State Fair was in session. The Kerr-Magee Company encouraged students to go to the fair. The students were to attend and write an essay called, "I Went To The Fair And This I Saw." Jan decided that she would enter the contest. She won a television for our classroom and a free lunch at the Hickory Inn. This was an elegant steakhouse. Teachers were invited to accompany the winners, but the students decided what the menu would be. We had hamburgers!

Our new television became a teaching tool. We studied French via television. The teacher was a very handsome man.

I remarked, "What a handsome man!" My students were appalled. The very idea! I was a married woman. I was not supposed to see any other man's attractiveness. I laughed and so did they. We continued our French lesson.

The next Sunday was Mother's Day. I was so touched and surprised when Sally and her high school brother brought me a gift.

Their mother was killed by the tornado. Their father's job kept him on the move. He was only home on the weekends. The brother accepted responsibility for Sally. Their gift to me was a tiny china basket. I kept that basket for years. It was lost in some move we made.

Sam and Jess lived on a farm. They rode the bus to school. They were always spick–and–span in appearance. These very clean boys had some traps set to catch animals. One morning just before the bus arrived, they visited a trap. They had an animal all right. It was a skunk. This very angry skunk took advantage of his chance for revenge. It sprayed these boys thoroughly. I don't know how the bus driver or the other children stood the awful scent. I knew they should not stay in those clothes all day. We were having a difficult time just having them in the room. I called their mother and explained the situation. She came immediately and took them home.

Philip was in the sixth grade and his brother, Luke, was in the fourth grade. I cannot remember the circumstances. Their mother may have been ill or she may have died. At any rate these two boys lived with their father. Philip assumed responsibility for keeping himself and Luke in clean clothes. He told me that he washed their clothes every night and ironed their shirts so they would look nice. He was not complaining. He seemed pleased that he could keep them looking clean.

Philip was an honor student. I hope the world treated both of the boys well. Sometimes, it is said that we earn the stars in our crown. Philip must have a crown surrounded by stars.

It was the first day of class. Kenneth came early and sat in the front row. He seemed ill at ease. Then he asked, "C-c-c-can you h-h-h-help m-m-m-me? I c-c-can't s-s-stop stuttering." This was so touching.

"I really don't know whether I can help you or not, " I answered.

"I-I-I c-c-can't e-e-even a-a-answer the t-t-telephone," he continued.

"Kenneth, try telling yourself that you will be able to answer the telephone before it rings. As you pick up the receiver, keep believing that you can answer."

Kenneth's mother asked, "What did you do to help Kenneth answer the telephone? Not only can he answer the telephone, he won't let anyone else answer it." We both rejoiced at this beginning for helping Kenneth gain confidence.

John was one of my students from the orphanage. He had a real struggle with math. His main interest was horses. He longed for a home that would let him have a horse. I decided that just maybe the horse would be the way to help John learn math. We worked together on adding and then subtracting horses. He even learned to multiply by using horses. Later, he was able to transfer this knowledge to other math problems that did not include his beloved horses.

We lived in Council Bluffs, Iowa, where I taught at Tinley School. My husband accepted a church that required him to be there in January. That meant that I would need to resign at midterm.

I'd had the privilege of supervising the honor students in a Kiwanis program. The boys were given honor uniforms. They stopped traffic so other students could cross streets safely. The girls assisted with supervision in the hallways and on the playgrounds. These students took their positions seriously. When they learned that I would be leaving, they and my colleagues decided to give me a special assembly.

Now, if you have never had a special assembly held in your honor, you cannot know how hard it is to keep your composure. I knew one tear would be one tear too many. The entire class would be in tears. I had to think of every funny thing I could think of to maintain control.

The weather gets cold in Council Bluffs. I was so pleased that the school had a gymnasium and that the students could run and play. They could make as much noise as they wanted as long as they did not endanger another student. This allowed them to work off their energy so they were ready to work when class convened.

There was an orphanage nearby, whose children attended our school. I, too, am an orphan, so I understood how much these children longed for love. It was interesting how they made a point of telling me that they were going home for lunch, but that they would come back to school. They would hunt for me and let me know when they returned. All of these children were not in my class.

TINLEY SCHOOL - GRADES 5 & 6
1957-58

I loved my students, but the students from the orphanage needed my love more than most. I became a surrogate mother to all of them.

My idea of teaching was that I could present any subject so that it was interesting and challenging. My purpose was not to see how many students I could fail. If they were failing, I was also failing. If they were failing, I wanted to know why. Sometimes, the student did not have the background for understanding the subject. Sometimes he lacked the study skills.

This is digressing from this age group, but it fits what I want to say. A class of graduate students was studying the basics for teaching children to read. The subject was phonics. One young woman said she already knew everything I was teaching. "Why don't we get on with something else?" My reply was, "You are going to prove to me that you can pass a test on the rules for teaching phonics. You are also going to show me you understand how to use a dictionary. I do not want you telling your students to look up a word in the dictionary without first teaching them how."

Several graduate students, including that young woman, had to take the test a second time because they did not know the rules sufficiently. I made time for them to come to my office and have another study review before retaking the test. This time they passed.

Longfellow School in Oklahoma City

Chapter 5

Teaching University Students

In July 2005, the bus and train system in London were bombed. I listened to the news to get the details. It seems the bombers were of Pakistani descent but had been working in London.

This brought back memories of turmoil in Iran in the 1970s, during the efforts to depose the Shah. Several of the students in one of my classes were from the Middle East. Some were Iranians, in favor of deposing the Shah; others supported the Shah. I suppose it was the natural thing for them to try to gain support from the American students.

My nephew fought in Vietnam. He said the major problem was not knowing who the enemy was. That was the case with the world situation in 2005. We had grown suspicious of those we did not know.

One of my Iranian students was absent whenever there was a march against the Shah. A friend would bring his excuse; usually something had happened to a close relative. One of the requirements for a grade was attendance. Work could not be completed outside of class. Students could make up missed classed, but they were not excused from attendance.

I called him to my desk when he returned from one of these absences. I told him I was not fooled by his stories. I read the papers and knew where he was. I told him I preferred honesty instead of excuses. He tried to persuade me to see his side of Iran's political problems. I assured him that I was not the least bit interested. I did not know enough about his country to understand the issues.

A very handsome Iranian student stood at my door. He had a single red rose in a vase. He asked me to forgive all of his countrymen for trying to impose their problems on me. I assured him that there was no problem. They would all be treated fairly.

In an earlier chapter, I mentioned that I'd once said to the Lord, "I asked you for a place to serve. If this is the place you want me, I need strength and courage to face each day."

Yes, he did answer that prayer. No one was more surprised than I when the University of Central Oklahoma asked me to fill in during another teacher's sabbatical the following year. That meant that I had to resign my current position. I was so excited that I went to my husband's office and shared the news with him. I asked, "Do you think I should go ahead and resign?" He was cautious. He told me that I should be very sure before handing in my resignation. I was to meet with the university's personnel committee the next morning.

The next morning, I told the chairman of the reading department that I had been asking myself over and over, "Did you really ask me to fill in during a sabbatical year?" He smiled and assured me that he had. We met that day with the committee. I shall never forget Dr. Joe Jackson adjusting his glasses, the better to watch me as I answered his questions. One of my recommendations had been from my history professor at Eastern Oklahoma Junior College, Dr. James Morrison. Dr. Jackson asked, "How well did you know Jimmy Morrison?"

"He was Dr. James Morrison to me," I replied. "I would never ever have called him Jimmy." Then I told Dr. Jackson and the committee how Dr. Morrison had been responsible for making sure that I was able to continue my education at Southeastern State College. I always suspected, but had no proof, that Dr. Morrison paid for my last two years at Southeastern State.

Dr. Jackson offered the job to me, and I accepted it. My new position permitted me to teach only undergraduates. One of my classes was called Developmental Reading. The purpose of this class was to help students improve their reading skills. What a thrill! I had the freedom to do what I most wanted to do.

Once again, I entered a room that was unkempt. Old tests and materials lay on shelves gathering dust. The bulletin board had information that was turning yellow with age. I asked the department chair if I might make some changes. She told me to make whatever changes I wished, including disposing of the out-of-date materials. The first thing I did was clean the room and make the bulletin board interesting and attractive. I also determined the requirements for earning two credit hours in this class. Long before I was hired, I had witnessed a student being turned away because the professor did not want to have any more students. Not only was the student turned away, she was rudely treated as well. I decided that would not happen in my relationship with the students.

I was surprised when the dean summoned me to his office to discuss Developmental Reading. Then he said, "I am told that the Greeks, the sororities and fraternities, take that class because it is an easy two hours."

"I have no way of knowing what was required by the former professor," I replied. "I do know that if anyone enrolls with that purpose in mind, they will drop the class. All students will earn their two hours."

He smiled. Then he welcomed me to the Department of Education and told me to sell the class.

I told the department chair about my conversation with the dean and asked if there was money available for a flyer. She assured me that there was but that no one had ever done one.

That did not dissuade me. I designed a flyer describing the class and gave it to the counselors and other staff who enrolled students. That gave the class a real boost. We had to add classes. I enjoyed seeing the progress of my students more than almost anything. They could read faster, comprehend what they read, and increase their vocabulary while enjoying the printed word.

It was spring. My first night class was in the basement of the Old North building. The class was full, so some of the students worked in an adjoining room. Everything was individualized so the divided class was not a problem. Neither was discipline. These students were paying to take the class, and they did not want to waste money. They were such a relief and so different from the students in my last teaching position.

A young man came to my desk and asked me to come with him. I followed him past the busy students. He went through the door leading into the hallway. He pointed to a snake that was not quite alert. It seemed to be trying to figure out where it was.

I asked the student if he was afraid of snakes. He said that he was. I told him to stay there and watch the snake while I went to my office and called the campus police. We were trying to keep everything as quiet as possible so the other students would not know about our visitor. The police arrived. They were equipped with guns and looked very foreboding.

They were accompanied by a gentleman who was a science professor. He wanted the snake. He and the policemen managed to pick up the snake and carry it outside. They placed it on the grass so they might get a good look. After determining that the snake was harmless, the professor reached down and grasped it behind the head. I was so glad that the story could end there. I had visions of the police shooting the snake.

Jessica was an excellent student. But she often was absent, and I could not figure out what had happened to her. One day, class was over and I was in my office. I heard a gentle knock, and there was Jessica. She asked if we might talk. Her roommate had committed suicide, and Jessica was having problems coping with the event. She talked about the effect the suicide had had on her. She thanked me for listening. I told her that she could come back if she felt that I could help. We made arrangements for her to make up the missed work. She said she thought that she could handle life again.

This class lasted for nine weeks. I explained to the students that during the class, I would remember their names and what they needed to improve in reading. I would do everything I could to help them reach their goal. However, at the end of their class, I would receive another class, so I might forget their names. "You should not feel bad if I cannot immediately recall your name," I said. "Tell me who you are." It was surprising how many times I was greeted by former students. They would explain how much they appreciated the skills they learned in Developmental Reading. We were friends.

Years earlier, I'd taught at a school where the faculty shunned me. One of those teachers was an art teacher named Sybil. I thought she was probably following the others and did not dare do otherwise. One of my university classes was called Teaching Reading Through the Content Areas. Sybil wanted to take this class. She came to me and hesitantly asked if she might enroll. I told her anyone who had the background to handle the subject matter was welcome. She seemed surprised that I would allow her to enroll.

She had a difficult time with the class. I asked her to make an appointment and let me give her some personal help. Maybe that would make things easier. We had taken a break during the three-hour class. She gasped and said, "Do you know what I want to do?"

I said, "No, what do you want to do?"

She replied, "I want to kiss you!"

I smiled and answered, "Go right ahead and kiss me."

She did. Then she said, "Now, I feel better."

I call that forgiveness. She brought me one of her paintings. I named it "Forgiveness."

In November 2005, I turned on the television and saw the news about a horrible bombing in Jordan. My mind immediately switched back to the year my Iranian students were taking sides for or against the Shah. Two handsome Jordanian students had come to my desk. They knew they resembled the Iranian students, which disturbed them. They wanted no part in Iran's political battle. One of them had purchased a new car. He was anxious to protect the car as well as himself. I did not know how to help them, but I could listen. One of the men said, "I am tempted to wear a name tag stating that I am from Jordan." Of course, he did not do this.

It makes me realize how sad it is that we judge all people from a race for the crimes of some. It has been years since I knew these fine young men. They are much older now. I hope all is well with them.

Idioms create a real problem for people learning the English language. An international student asked me, "What do my friends mean when they say that I am 'sitting on a fence'? I am not on a fence." I explained that they meant he was not choosing a side.

I found it interesting that even a gray-haired teacher had to be careful when working with other adults. A handsome young airman tried to impress me with a bit of surprising attention. I reminded him, "Don't forget who you are. You are the student and I am the teacher." Everything worked out just fine.

This class was individualized. Tests determined a starting place. I had had experience designing such classes at the junior-high level. Each student had information concerning class requirements in his or her own folder, which contained materials and the way to meet those requirements. The student would pick up the folder and do the work listed inside. It was my job to help where needed.

One evening, a student sat watching me. I wondered why she had not started working, so I asked if she needed help. She said, "No, I find this positively amazing. You know what everyone is doing. This is so well planned, I cannot believe it."

Students sometimes audited the class to obtain some special skill. A forty-six-year-old man wanted to learn to spell. He was convinced that he could not spell because he was dyslexic. He could read the most complicated articles concerning dyslexia. This told me that his problem was something else.

I asked him to come to my desk for individual instruction. He was trembling as he said, "You do not understand. I am very dyslexic."

"No, I understand that you are afraid to learn to spell," I answered.

Then he asked, "Are you going to give me baby words?"

"Are you a baby?"

He answered, "No."

I explained, "We will start with short words and work up to larger words."

I used the Glass Analysis system, which focused on word parts. I told him the word part while holding the card in front of him. He repeated what I said. We then reversed the order until we had worked through the list. I asked him to open his notebook for his first spelling test. Terror filled his face. I said the word. It was not a small word. He wrote the word. I turned the card around for him to grade himself. His word was correct. His fist banged my desk so loudly that the other students looked up. He said, "Why did I have to wait until I was forty-six to find someone who could teach me to spell?" Every word was spelled correctly. He was so pleased and so was I.

I remember teaching a fourth grader who had reading problems. He was so ashamed when he graded his spelling paper. I took him aside and told him that he should try to spell one more word correctly each day. Spelling would always be difficult, but he could improve with that goal. This was something he could do. Teachers are always learning. Dr. Glass had not perfected his word cluster program at that time. Now, I believe that I could have given that fourth grader success in spelling through using Glass Analysis.

Having students write their misspelled word several times over always seemed so ridiculous to me. Another thing that has always irritated me is telling the student, "You just aren't studying enough." Students have to be led through a lesson for it to have real meaning.

Robert came to the university seeking help with reading. He was dressed like a person who was doing well financially. His demeanor did not display the way he felt about himself. He had heard about the reading department and its excellent work. He said he had prayed, asked God to guide him to the people who might help him. He was led to the university.

Our department chair wanted to work with him, and she did for a year, and then she let someone else try teaching him. The man's second professor was one of the best. She had a lot of knowledge and patience, but she, too, gave up. Our chair called me in. "Will you take Robert?" she asked. I was most happy to have the challenge. I had wanted to teach Robert from the time he first arrived. I believed strongly in God, and I also had worked with a number of adults with reading problems.

The first thing I did was find out about his background. He had a brother who read quite well, which made Robert feel inferior. Robert's wife was a wonderful lady. She helped him as much as she could. They were financially well off but that did not substitute for Robert's lack of self-esteem. Robert wanted to read.

We started at the beginning. I taught him the same word list that first graders learn. These he would memorize. I used Glass Analysis to help him learn word parts. This is a good system because the student and teacher work through words together. We started with the starter set and progressed to the next levels of difficulty. We used the same lists for spelling.

Oral reading was a must. I liked the book, "A Walk Across America." It is an adult story. It is exciting to see the hero grow as he sees America. Robert would guide me as I read a few sentences. Then I would guide him as he read the same sentences. Sometimes, I would find a magazine with interesting information. He enjoyed this because it allowed him to be informed. He could discuss the information with others. Newspapers were good reading sources. I picked our reading materials carefully.

Robert soon was ready to learn comprehension skills. We had several levels of materials for teaching these skills. He learned the importance of words like where, when, why, what, which, and how. I had to lead him through everything, but he was learning.

One morning, he was doing really well. I suddenly realized that Robert could read. It was like a miracle. I did not want to startle him, so I said nothing. The next day he was doing even better. I asked him, "Do you know what has happened to you?"

He smiled and answered, "Yes, I do."

"How do you know?" I asked.

He replied, "I can read the street sign. I can read the advertisements on the billboards. I can divide any of the words."

"Are you happy with your newfound skills?"

"Really, I am a bit frightened," he said.

"You wanted to learn to read. Why does it bother you now that you can read?"

His answer surprised me. He said, "I am happy that I can read, but now I must be responsible for everything. Someone else has always done that for me."

Teresa was a beautiful black woman. I first met her when she was a student in Developmental Reading. She had a slight hearing problem, which was enough to create insecurity. She was willing to try, and that made my job to help her much easier. She passed the course with a very good grade.

The next time we met she was taking a course called Lab for Reading Disabilities. She was a natural teacher. Her demeanor and her skill in planning for her own class was a joy to observe. One day, when I was working with other students, I suggested that they visit with Teresa and see how she planned her work. This, they did.

Then one day after she had completed the Lab course she came to the Developmental Reading class. She said, "I need some advice. I am enrolled in a class for Learning Disabilities. The professor wants us to ask questions. I know the answers, so I do not talk. There are only a dozen students in the class. What am I going to do?"

"Teresa, most of us go through this same problem," I told her. "You are going to ask the questions even though you know the answers. You will get used to hearing your voice."

She graduated with honors. One night as I was teaching a rather large class, I heard a tapping on my door. I asked the students to excuse me for a few moments. When I opened the door, there stood Teresa. She had a big smile on her face. "I just had to let you know that I have a job!"

She also was taking night classes in preparation for a master's degree. Every teacher should have the privilege of teaching a Teresa.

My first night class in Old North was the only class in that part of the building. The class was large. A young man remained after almost everyone else had left. He said that he wanted to talk with me. An older student also waited. I told the young man he should make an appointment and I would be happy to see him in my office. Finally, the younger man left. The other gentleman asked, "May I help you lock up?" I welcomed his help. He walked me to my car. The next time the class met, the man who walked me to the car come to my desk. He said, "I think I should introduce myself. I am a policeman with Oklahoma City. I did not feel good about you being alone with that other student."

Neither of us knew it, but that student had just been released from prison. He did not come back to class. I have felt bad about that. On one hand, perhaps I could have helped him resolve whatever was bothering him. On the other hand, it might not have been safe for me.

A handsome young man from a prominent family was enrolled in Developmental Reading. He knew the requirements for passing the course. Every student was given daily assignments that fit his or her particular need. I was always there to assist them. This student chose to ignore requirements. He seemed to think his place in society would be enough. Failing a student has always been difficult for me. The old saying, "You can lead a horse to water, but you cannot make him drink" fits this situation.

Visitors were not welcomed in Developmental Reading. There was no room. We did not want any distractions. One day, about midway through the semester, a young man came to class.

I asked him if he were a visitor. He gave me a vague answer. I was polite but explained our situation. He left. Later I learned that he had enrolled in the class but had never attended. He was on the football team. I felt bad about the situation, but at that stage of the semester there was no way he could have completed the requirements.

One of my roles in the reading department was to supervise a class called Lab for Reading Disabilities. Children who were behind in their class could enroll for remediation in reading or other subjects. The graduate students working toward a master's degree in reading became their teachers.

Jerome was one of these children. His basic problem was math. He could read the problem and even understand the requirements, but he worked very slowly. One afternoon I was checking his work. He greeted me with a beautiful smile. I returned the smile and asked, "How was your day?"

He became very sad. "Well, actually, I got in trouble in school. I even got swats."

"Would you like to tell me what happened?"

He said, "The teacher has us work problems as fast as we can. I am always late."

I told him that I might have a solution if he would like to try it. He agreed that he was willing to try something different. I brought him my stopwatch and showed him how to use it. He could time himself.

The stopwatch was like having a toy. He would take a sheet of math. Then he would turn off the watch and work against it. He mastered the problem before very long. He was a much happier young man.

My husband and I ran a Student Center for our Presbyterian Church. Our students took classes at Southeastern State College and were transported from the center to the college by bus. One of them was Faye, who came from a small high school. She was an excellent student, so you can understand how devastated she was when she received a low grade on a theme. "I just knew it!" she said, "I am not college material."

I replied, "Now, wait a minute. One down does not mean always down!"

She said, "Okay, but how I am supposed to write a two hundred word theme on Robert Frost's 'Stopping By Woods on a Snowy Evening.' The theme is to be on the last verse of his poem. Now, I ask you, how am I going to do that?"

"I just happen to have a little free time," I answered. "Come into our dining room and let's take a look at your assignment." We read the poem together. Then I asked her to read it again.

"This time read only the verse. Who is this person who stopped by the snowy woods?"

She looked at me. It was like a light had come on. She said, "Why, it is a country doctor."

I asked, "Why did he stop?"

"He has just come from a very difficult case," she answered. "The woman will die if he cannot figure out a way to help her!"

I continued asking her questions to stimulate her thinking. Then I left her to write her theme. I checked back, and she was still writing. She enthusiastically wrote her theme. And yes, she got an A. She became a wonderful teacher.

Old North Building

The New Department of Education

Chapter 6

Teaching Special Programs

It was my privilege to teach language arts in Oklahoma's first Manpower Program. The students were young men ages eighteen to twenty-one, who for some reason had not completed high school. They were tested, and their scores determined their placement in this special federal program. This program was based at Southeastern State University and housed at Oklahoma Presbyterian Center in Durant, Oklahoma.

These fifty young men were divided into three groups. One group attended language arts. Another group took a math class, and the third group was in a mechanics program. The math and language arts classes were taught at the Oklahoma Presbyterian Center. These men attended classes all day.

What an assortment of students they were. These were the black-jacket, cigarette-hanging-from-the-mouth days. The smoking was quickly forbidden. They came swaggering into the class on the first day, a pose that told me: "I am feeling very insecure. I want you to think I really know who I am, but I really do not."

These students ranged from the non-readers all the way to the ones who could read some. Most were below grade level. One young man obviously did not belong in the group. After we became acquainted, I asked him, "Why are you here? We both know that you are well ahead of all of these men." He gave me a twisted grin and answered, "Well, you see, I goofed up in high school and became a dropout. I grew up some and really wanted to complete high school, but I did not want to go back to regular high school."

"How did you get into this program?"

He smiled and said, "Well, I knew what kind of grade I needed to make on the test."

My next question was, "Will you go on to college when you complete this program?"

He replied, "That is my goal."

When I look back, I wish there were other programs that could pick up some more of these young men and help them find their way. It grieves me to see so many destroying themselves with drugs and general misbehavior.

Tests determined placement. Leroy was a non-reader, so we started as though he were a first grader. I have always admired people like Leroy who are willing to admit that they need help. The men in the program were somewhat hardened to the world as they saw it. They knew they had failed regular education programs. It was a delight to see how helpful they were to Leroy. He did not hesitate going to one of them when he did not know a word. I do not remember, but I would guess Leroy was dyslexic.

The shop class was on the Southeastern State College campus. One day Robert came to me with a complaint. He said, "We do not like the way the college students treat us."

I asked, "How is that?"

"Oh, they act like we are stupid or don't know anything."

I replied, "Why do you suppose that happens? You are the same age. You are quite handsome. What makes the college students treat you that way? Is there anything you could do to cause them to think differently?"

He sat quietly and thought about what I had said. Then he smiled and answered, "Yes, I think we can. I will call a meeting, and we will talk about it. Maybe if we dressed differently and cleaned up, it might help."

Indeed it did. Not only were the men treated well, two of them ended up marrying college graduates. One of the men was severely dyslexic, but he was a good mechanic. He was a regular Mr. Charming. He married an elementary school teacher, who could read for him and help him where he needed it most. That was a real thrill. His name was Charles. He was always saying to me, "How about going to dinner with me?"

I would answer, "Okay, when shall we do this?"

He would smile and, "One of these days." This went on the whole semester. Class was over and I was putting away materials. There was Charles with his precious smile. He asked, "Well, are you going to dinner with me?"

"Sure, when are we going?"

He said, "How about tonight? I want you and Mr. Poe to have dinner at my folks' farm. The other teachers are coming, too."

What a treat that was! You have not had fried chicken until you have tasted chicken cooked by a wonderful farm wife. We had the chicken plus all of the trimmings. After that, I told my husband that I would never again worry about Charles. He was surrounded by the love of a wonderful family plus a beautiful wife. He also had a job, so he could make a living. Now, that is what every teacher hopes for as she helps each student find his way.

Control is so important in a well-run classroom. I learned early on that a sense of humor was another vital requirement. One new student came to the Manpower class. He set about disturbing the other students and trying to stir up trouble. I made the horrible mistake of becoming angry, which meant that he had won. I went to my husband's office and told him what had happened. I was so angry with myself for losing control. I said, "That will not happen again!" And it didn't.

The Oklahoma Presbyterian Center housed both college students and people who came from other countries to explore the possibilities of college. Rebecca was from Mexico. What a beautiful lady she was! She wanted to learn the English language. She tried enrolling in high school, but she was turned away and was upset about this. I said, "You are welcome to attend the Manpower Program." She was shocked. She answered, "There are only men there?" I said, "Well, no, that is not true. I am there." She agreed that she would attend our classes. She did wonders for the men. Not only was she pretty, she was smart. I could not have found better motivation for them. Rebecca was all business. She was there to learn. The men could not have a woman do more than they did. They really went to work.

They did object to calling out to a woman in an all-men's class. They decided that she should be called George. That made everything all right.

Robert and Joe were brothers. They came from a small town. I am not sure why they had dropped out of school. It was evident that they came from a fine caring family. They were good students who made the most of the program. Hopefully, they gained enough help to allow them to find good jobs. They were achievers, so I am sure they now have good homes in some town of their choice.

One day, we discussed why they were in such a program. One fine-looking young man said, "I just got so smart the teachers could not teach me." The bitterness was not directed at the teachers but at himself.

The whole purpose of this program was to help these men qualify for a job. Letter writing and a command of English were most important. They also were taught how write a resume. A neat and clean appearance was stressed.

Manpower Program

We decided to do a play-acting demonstration of someone applying for a job. Each student was scheduled to come to an office and talk with a person looking to fill a position. They took this very seriously. They dressed in suits and were unbelievably handsome. Their demeanor was perfect as they approached the hoped-for boss. I was so proud of them. Hopefully, this helped them find a job that was just right for them.

My husband spent the last twelve years of his career as a vocational rehabilitation counselor. He was a good one. He told me about a young man, sort of the hippie type, who wanted to become a plumber. This man was an excellent student and graduated with honors. He saw an ad in the paper. He applied for the job and was turned down. He came to see my husband. He was livid. He said, "I know that job was open. Why did they refuse to hire me?" My husband did not answer. He waited. The man asked, "Do you think it was it was my appearance?"

"That's possible," my husband answered.

The young man became angry. He said, "Well, that is my right. I can dress any way I want!"

My husband agreed. He replied, "You are correct. But it is also the employing person's right not to hire you." Then he explained to the plumber that he would be going into homes where women were alone. They might be afraid of someone who looked scraggly.

This story has a wonderful ending. The young man went out and bought new clothes. He cut his hair and generally cleaned up. He went to the same place, applied, and this time got the job. Later he started his own plumbing business. I wonder what his dress requirements were for the men he employed.

This is not my personal experience, but it shows the type of goal my Manpower students were working toward. These men were housed in the same dormitory as our college students. We were proud of the grounds and the buildings. Things changed when these men moved in. We had to become stricter.

One day I set out to make my Manpower students angry. That is not a recommended approach, but it did work. I started the class by saying, "I have decided that people who drink beer have no pride." Immediately, the students were on the defensive. "How can you say that?"

"Well, before you came to live here our grounds were neat, and we were so proud of them. Now, we must go around picking up beer cans that you have thrown here and there. It does not seem too difficult to carry an empty beer can to a garbage can. I just don't understand the mindset of people who expect others to pick up after them."

The discussion ended, and we began our work. No more trash or beer cans littered our beautiful ground or buildings. The students took pride in where they lived.

Oklahoma Presbyterian Center, Durant, Oklahoma

OPC Students

It was my privilege to work with Oklahoma University in an Upward Bound Program over the course of two summers. This program helps young people prepare for college. The first of these was held at an agricultural Experiment Station in Madill, Oklahoma. I suppose the university officials thought it would be easier to control the students there.

An alligator was in a large vat just outside of the dining area. My students were told not to put anything in the vat, but the girls could not resist. They dropped paper napkins and other debris in the vat. One night the stillness was shattered by the girls' screaming. It seems that the plugged-up vat had overflowed, allowing the alligator to float out. The girls heard swish, swish, swish. They looked and saw the alligator heading for their rooms. The caretaker hurriedly caught the alligator and returned it to the now clean vat. Need I say, the girls not longer teased the alligator.

Sometimes there were special programs. Because my class was in session, I did not attend Doc Tate's special presentation of his Indian flute. Doc Tate was a Cheyenne Indian who was known for making and playing the Indian flute. "I did not get to hear you play," I complained to him. "I was teaching."

Doc Tate said, "Don't worry, I will come to your room and give a special program."

We agreed on a time. I hurriedly found several people who could join me for the program. He was true to his word. We all felt very special to receive such treatment.

The next summer I was asked to do another Upward Bound Program with the university. This time the classes would be on the university campus. I was so pleased that I'd had the previous summer to become acquainted with many of the faculty. Those relationships came in handy. As I was busy organizing the program and hurrying to get to my own classes, I had not taken the time to get a parking sticker. I came out to find a ticket on my car. I hurried to the administration offices to see what could be done. These men knew me and got quite a charge out of my getting a ticket.

Dr. Webber said, "Okay, bring me the ticket and I will take care of it." They were just wonderful to me.

Many years later, Dr. Morris, vice president at Oklahoma University, was the commencement speaker when I received my master's degree from the University of Central Oklahoma. I wondered if he would remember me. When the university president called my name, Dr. Morris looked up and smiled. As I moved on down the line, he got up and stopped the line so he could congratulate me. How very nice to have friends like him.

Students in the Upward Bound and similar programs often did not have high-school diplomas. Furthermore, many of the enrollees were troublemakers. Two black girls were determined to stir up problems. Every day, I had to spend some unnecessary time getting them to work. One day they arrived with a boom box.

"Why are you girls in this program?" I asked.

One of the answered, "Oh, we wanted to learn to read."

"Really! That is why you are here?" I asked. "Then, why don't you do what I ask?"

They looked at each other, grinned, and said, "Okay, we will do it."

What a shame. I had just gotten them to work well for me when the director told me they had been expelled. They had attacked the English teacher. I can appreciate the teacher's exasperation with their attitude, but I felt bad about losing them.

Most of the Upward Bound students worked hard to make up for lost time. I would like to believe that many of them returned to school with a different attitude, once they had set some better goals for themselves.

I did a third Upward Bound Program with returning veterans at Oscar Rose Junior College in Midwest City, Oklahoma. This was a night class with young men who had just returned from serving in the armed forces.

I walked into the room with my arms full of tests. You should have seen their faces!

"Are you going to give us a test?" one of them asked.

'Well, I thought I would, but let's talk about it. You see, the tests will show where you are, so that the program I plan for you fits your needs. I don't really need the tests for myself, but I thought you would like to know. This test is not for a grade. It is for placement. You will take another one at the end of the semester to show how much progress you have made. Now, do we take the test or not? It is up to you."

We voted. Everyone agreed to take the test.

They wanted an open grade book. I told them that fine with me. If they did not care who saw their grades, I didn't. So we had an open grade book. They checked often to see their standings. Sometimes one of them would request more work in an area in which he was weak.

This was a most satisfying project. Their progress was amazing. They were so proud of themselves, and so was the director of the program. He posted their scores for everyone to see.

One of the veterans came from the same area I did. His name was unusual. When I called the roll that first night, he looked at me and asked, "Now, how did you know how to say my name? No one else pronounces it correctly."

"See me at the break, and I will tell you," I said. He stopped to visit. I told him that I knew his family, and that they had enjoyed coming to activities where I lived and stirring up fights. He smiled and replied, "Well, we have changed. We decided we should go to college and work like other people."

I also moonlighted at Oklahoma's Tinker Air Base. This was fascinating. The airmen came for help if they felt they needed it. The teachers never knew who the students would be. They were always gentlemen.

One young pilot told me that while he could read, he did not understand much of what he read. I asked him to read out loud. It turned out that he was skipping the middle of large words, which caused them to lose their meaning. I asked him to allow me to guide him as he read. I placed a plain index card under the sentence and moved it slowly. He read perfectly. He asked, "Now, why did that make a difference?" I explained that he had a tracking problem. His eyes were skipping over the middle of words that were three or more syllables. It was such a simple problem, and it had a simple solution. I told him using a guide might improve his comprehension.

There are many teachers who could solve a student's problem if they could work individually with that person.

Chapter 7

Workshops

When I was still a new teacher in the university's reading department, the department chair said, "Edith, it is your turn to do a workshop." naïvely I asked, "What would you like me to do in the workshop?" She smiled and said, "That is your decision." I discovered that teaching at the university level was different from teaching in the public schools. In the public schools, the teacher consulted a curriculum guide and the chosen textbook. At the university, the professor determined what would be taught. In this case, the workshop subject was selected by the professor, and an outside consultant would be hired to present the new ideas to the students.

Where to begin? I went to my professional books, especially those I'd received from the International Reading Association. There I found a topic that had special interest for me. Like everything else, people continue to find new ways to deal with the subject of reading. "Reading in the content area," i.e., science, history, and social studies, had an appealing sound. I read and read and took note of the people who were publishing articles on the topic. We were permitted to have an outside consultant. I was fortunate to find a professor from Tempe, Arizona, who had published findings about his research in reading in the content areas.

The next step was to find out if this professor was available for a summer workshop focused on reading in the content areas. I checked the dates for the workshop on our summer calendar and then got in touch with the professor. We discussed my ideas and decided that this workshop could be done.

The professor was able to come for the week. Now, I had to sell the workshop. I set about designing a flyer that I could make available to students looking for summer classes.

I found this exciting and challenging. It was amazing how many graduate students were interested in the subject. The workshop sold out. The professor lived up to my expectations and provided a most interesting learning experience.

This caused me to look further into teaching reading in the content area. Eventually, I wrote a course on the topic.

Children entering third grade sometimes have difficulty understanding the subject matter of science, social studies, geography, and history. These same subjects have been presented in story form in grades one and two. But later they are taught in an informational form. Current textbook writers are doing a better job of presentation. Usually, they offer a lesson preview as a lead in to studying.

Too many times, the teacher working with these subject areas has no training in the ways to make content area classes easier. Often, the teacher tells the students to read and answer the questions at the end of the chapter. An emphasis on study skills is most important. These study skills can make learning more interesting and should precede the reading of the chapter. Ask the student to:

1. Read the chapter title.
2. Read the chapter outline (if one is present).
3. Look carefully at all illustrations. (These are not fillers. They are there to help the student have a better understanding of the subject.)
4. Study any word printed differently from the text. Some may be darker or have a different style of printing.
5. Read the questions at the end of the chapter.

I was leading a class through study skills. I explained that the questions at the end of the chapter should be read first. One student said, "No, we are not supposed to do that." He considered that cheating. I assured him that he was mistaken. If you read the questions first, you know what the author wants you to remember, and you can search for the answers as you read.

Another workshop dealt with the decoding of words using the Glass Analysis System. Teachers are always looking for new ways to present this skill. Phonics has long been the primary tool. Economy Phonics does an excellent job of teaching word recognition, and I liked using this system. In Economy Phonics, the vowels are presented first, the long vowel sound first and then the short vowel sounds. While the students are learning the vowel sounds, they are also learning the consonants.

Dr. Gerald Glass had four levels of word clusters for teaching decoding. The first level is called Starters; these clusters work with the vowel sounds. This is what I used with the forty-six year old man who audited the Developmental Reading class at the University of Central Oklahoma. He was the one who asked if I was going to give him baby words. I told him that while it would be necessary to start with small words, we would progress to harder words within the same lesson. He was overjoyed when he was able to spell two and three syllable words correctly. Dr. Glass's program made it easier to teach older students.

Dr. Glass called the next three levels of word clusters Mediums, Harders, and Completers. The spelling words become more difficult with each level. This workshop was popular. I had not problem promoting it.

A fellow faculty member, Dr. Mitchell, taught a workshop on Adult Basic Education. He invited me to help with that workshop. I enjoyed doing this. I already had experience in teaching adults.

One of my students was an elderly Choctaw Indian woman. She came to my desk and said, "Edith, I knew your father." Unless you are an orphan who has very little knowledge of your father, you cannot appreciate what this meant to me. My father died when I was five years old. I remembered a few things about him, but not many. I asked her to have lunch with me and tell me about my father. What a blessing that was!

The adult basic education workshops soon became routine. I did one every summer and thoroughly enjoyed working with the graduate students and other adults who attended them.

Chapter 8

Tutoring

Why is tutoring such a passion for me?

The renewed interest in tutoring programs thrills me. Experience has taught me that one–on–one or small group tutoring can make a difference between poverty and a better life.

Education was so important to me. I was caught in a situation that held very little promise for anything beyond high school. My parents both died by the time I was nine years old. My mother's sister took the three of us and reared us as her children. I shall always be grateful to her for keeping us in school.

She believed high school was enough. No one in our family had gone to college.

She said, "You will just get married anyway." She was right. I did marry, but not until I had a bachelor's degree.

I married O. Dixon Poe. He became a Presbyterian Minister and we moved a lot.

One of the places we lived was Woodward, Oklahoma. This is where I first tutored.

Our daughter became ill. I resigned my position with the school and stayed home with her. The principal called me and asked if I would tutor a high school student who would fail without help. I told him I would be happy to tutor her if she could come to my home. This was the beginning. Before the semester was over I had more students than I had time. This worked out well for me, because my baby daughter was in the room with us.

The first student was a Methodist Minister's daughter. She was such a lovely young lady. Perhaps being moved as Methodist Ministers are created some of her problems. She worked well with me and was able to graduate.

She also graduated from Tulsa University. Wouldn't that have been a waste for her to fail in high school?

One of my students for tutoring was a Polish lady. She was working for a family. She wanted to become an American citizen. Sometimes I would move a little fast for her. She would remind me that she was not young. She successfully passed the test for citizenship. I received a beautiful red, white, and blue floral arrangement as a thank you. She asked if I thought it would be all right to send an arrangement to her church. I believe she was Lutheran. I told her to call the church and ask. I feel certain they would appreciate her achievement as much as I did.

People who needed assistance in learning to read seemed to find me. I did not advertise. One student was a first grader in our church. I have told his story in my chapter about First Graders, but I would like to repeat some of it here.

His mother was convinced that her son was behind because he was in the Sparrows Group. She begged me to tutor him. I agreed. She discovered that her son was in the accelerated group. So you see even Sparrows can fly.

Another first grader was young for his class. I have told you his story also in the same chapter.

It was interesting that his teacher felt there was no way for him to catch up. That was when his mother came to see me. He was most receptive to my teaching and was soon leading his class. The teacher begged his mother to take him out of tutoring. She didn't.

I have told you about another student, a girl, who was a late-in-life child. She had grown siblings. They all adored her. She had complete control of her family, but this presented a problem when she enrolled in first grade. The counselor and her teacher called the parents in for a discussion of the problem. They felt she was too immature to complete the first grade in one year.

The parents brought her to Bella Vista Community Church Tutoring Program. I had started this program and was the director. I agreed to be the tutor for this child. Long ago I had learned that you place a child like this in no compromising position.

You also keep her interest by changing from one skill to another so that she has no time for boredom. She was delightful. She was sharp and thrilled to be learning. We studied the Sight Words. These words are called The Dolch Sight Words. These are words most frequently used in all reading.

You have read Julie's story in the chapter about first graders. The point is, without tutoring, Julie would have repeated first grade.

The University of Central Oklahoma had a class for teaching teachers how to work with reading disabilities. Children from the communities near the university enrolled for the class. Teachers working toward master's degrees became their teachers.

The Reading Professors each had charge of some of these graduate students.

One gentleman came to me after reading his student's folder. He said, "Look at this. It says that this student will probably never do any better than this. What do you think about that?"

I replied, "I always teach to win. I suggest that you do the same."

He smiled and said, "Will do!"

His student improved far beyond the prediction. All of us rejoiced.

So far, you have heard mostly about young children. It is surprising how many adults can profit from tutoring. I told you about Robert in the chapter about university students. Adults have a difficult time giving the time required to overcome a severe reading problem. You may remember that Robert worked for three years before he could read. He worked with three very well qualified professors. When the breakthrough came it was both interesting and alarming for Robert. Now he had to be responsible for himself. He found this frightening.

The mature nonreader has found ways to cope with the disability. Sometimes they can surprise everybody.

A minister's daughter was sent to me for tutoring. Her mother realized that her daughter could read or at least she could say the words. She could not retain the meaning of what she had read. Maxine was sent in the hopes that I might help her process what she read. Her sister was to be married that spring. She was marrying a man from one of the Eastern states.

I thought maybe studying about Robert Frost might give her some understanding of the area. Her sister would be living in that part of our country. She seemed interested and enjoyed discussing the poetry.

We continued reading about some other well-known people. One day I asked her mother what Maxine was saying about the class. She said, "She says you are just studying about some old dead people."

I decided to read about Thomas Edison. She thoroughly enjoyed the story. I asked her why it mattered that Edison had lived. Did she have any reason to care whether he did or didn't live? She looked at me and grinned. "Well, the electric light makes it much easier for all of us in many ways."

Maxine made progress, but not enough. We learned that the College of the Ozarks in Clarksville, Arkansas, had a special division for working with dyslexics. Her lack of ability to process what she read was a form of dyslexia. She graduated from Clarksville and I am sure that she did well in life.

When I was working on my master's degree, a psychology professor asked, "How many of you skipped a grade?" I was one of those students. I was far ahead of the class when we came to live with my Aunt Elsie. This was a time when accelerated students were moved up a class. Of course that no longer happens, because there are classes for the accelerated student.

Later, this professor asked me to teach for him. He had a private clinic. It was here that I met Paul. I shall never forget seeing this fine young man with his head bowed down. He was dirty and smelly. I asked, "Are you really so frightened?"

"Yes, you are my last chance! I am supposed to be graduating from high school. No one is fooling me. I cannot read. They are just pushing me out. I want to be able to make a living and someday have a wife and family. What is going to happen to me?"

"So we know the problem, I answered. I told him that was a good way to start.

I always found that a student learned better through working with something that was of special interest to him. So we visited. He had dreams of customizing cars. He wanted to be able to attend a Technical School in Okmulgee, Oklahoma.

The next lesson I brought a copy of *Car and Driver*. I taught words that could help him develop a vocabulary for his interest. We did oral reading. Often I would let him pick an article he would like to read. First, I would ask him to follow as I read to him. Then I would have him read the part I had just read to him. The procedure worked very well. It was slow, but it worked enough that he felt a sense of improvement.

As the classes progressed Paul began to feel better about himself. He cleaned up. He bathed and washed his hair. He came well-groomed. I complimented him on his appearance.

He was a handsome young man. He no longer felt rejected.

The teaching of reading is like everything else. New ideas are presented. Dr. Gerald Glass's Glass Analysis in one of the best for decoding. The Economy Phonics program is excellent but moves slower than the Dr. Glass method. How I wish that I had known about Glass Analysis when I was teaching Paul. This program calls for student feedback. It is amazing how quickly students pick up word patterns. Spelling grades improve decidedly.

I met some interesting students while tutoring for the psychologist. One was a girl that I will call Helen. Helen was in the seventh grade. She was struggling with more than one problem. She was overweight and very much worried about displeasing her mother. As we did oral reading I noticed that she could read fairly well, but she often missed little words like "was."

This became a pattern. One day I asked her, "Who told you that you cannot even do the small words?" The terrified look that came in her eyes revealed that I was right in assuming that she experienced that very thing.

Now, it was my challenge to help her overcome this "spell" that had been cast on her.

Before we started oral reading I assured her that she was capable of overcoming this thing that troubled her. Like the "stutterer" who could not answer the telephone, she needed to tell herself that the little words were not a problem. She continued stumbling as she approached the smaller words. We made up a game. As she read orally she made points for moving smoothly over the small words. We kept working on overcoming the way she felt about herself. She eventually succeeded. It was a joy to see her smile when she had done well.

All of us who work with children should remember that we injure children with cruel words. It breaks my heart to hear a parent tell a child, "Oh, you are so stupid."

Years ago I had the privilege of hearing S. I. Hayakawa speak on the subject, "Change Starts From Within." He refers to a book by Prescott Lecky called *Self Consistency: A Theory of Personality.* The book was published in 1945 and is long out of print. In this book Preston Lecky asks, "What is the matter with the bright student who excels in all subjects, but cannot learn to spell?"

Lecky suggests an answer. "This deficiency is not due to lack of ability, but rather to an active resistance which prevents him learning how to spell in spite of extra instruction. The resistance arises from the fact that at some time in the past the suggestion that he is a poor speller was accepted and incorporated into his definition of himself."

If he defines himself as a poor speller, the misspelling of a certain portion of the words he used becomes for him a moral issue. The student who audited my reading class believed he would never learn to spell. When he was proven wrong he was simply overcome with his success. He had overcome a stumbling block that he had lived with for forty-six years. Again it was a very real treat to see him succeed where he had failed for years.

The man who married my aunt thought of himself as strong in math. One night I was doing my homework. He wanted to see what I was doing. Then he proceeded to tell me how I should be working the math. Math is like reading. Ways of teaching math change, so I was not working the math as he remembered. He had a very short fuse. He was soon cursing me and telling me how dumb I was. This had a lasting effect on my life until I became an adult and realized what he had done to me. I was actually afraid to take math in college, so I took foreign language to fulfill that requirement. I am quite good at math, but I did not know that.

Dr. Hayakawa's lecture was called, "Crush Starts Early." He used an illustration of a kindergarten teacher who planned very carefully some Easter baskets the children would make.

She gave the children the materials and instructions on the way the baskets were to be made. She was horrified when one little boy wanted to turn the decorative pieces sideways instead of putting them erect as she had planned. She even had him take the pieces off and arrange them as she wanted. When she moved away the boy put three pieces as instructed, but he put one of them as he wanted. The teacher was not happy about what he had done.

Another student cut up the handle. She could not get the handle to stay on. The teacher wanted to know why she had destroyed the handle and cut up the other decorations and pasted them on the basket. The child said, "Well, I guess I do not want a handle. The teacher's reply: "Oh, you spoiled yours. Yours is all messy and doesn't have a handle."

Another professor reviewing the situation was on the children's side. He says the two students who did the baskets differently were thinking for themselves.

This made me remember my own son. We attended an Open House for parents to see the child's work. His teacher greeted us with, "You will find his work done quite well, but it will have his individual touch." We deeply appreciated this wonderful teacher who did not squelch our son's creativeness.

This teacher did another motivational thing that caused the accelerated student to enjoy learning. She had an especially beautiful box filled with all kinds of things the student could do.

First, the assigned work must be done well. The student then had the privilege of going to this box and choosing something that interested him. This, too, had to be done well. Then the finished work was placed in a basket for extra credit.

Bob was fifty-six years old when his wife died. His daughter asked, "Dad, isn't there something you always wanted to do, but never had the time?" She must have been surprised when he replied, "Yes, there is. I have always wanted to learn to read." At this time I had my own Tutoring Business. So Bob came to enroll in our tutoring program. I became Bob's tutor.

Bob was a machinist. Apparently, he was a very good machinist. He was also a good businessman. He owned property in Oklahoma City and a cabin on a lake. I do not know how much his daughter knew about her father's disability.

It was a complete surprise to me. Bob knew the letters of the alphabet, but he had not the foggiest idea of letter sounds. We worked on the letter sounds for several lessons. He first learned the m sound. Then he wanted to start all words with the m sound. He had a keen sense of humor. This helped us both.

Bob literally had to start like a first grader. He didn't mind. So we worked on the Sight Words. We also used Glass Analysis. We did oral reading. I had him follow me as I read a sentence. Then he would read the same sentence. As he progressed we could extend the amount of reading he could do. He was delighted with every bit of progress. So many times a learning disabled adult becomes discouraged, because he cannot learn immediately. Often times they quit. Not Bob; he was there for every class. He did make some progress. Then his company transferred him to another state. He insisted that he would continue working on reading. My hope is that he found someone who could help him.

Jim was a fourth grader. He was talented in anything having to do with machines. He worked with his father in his shop. Machines were fascinating. But the teacher wanted him to write a poem about kites. The assignment was not interesting to Jim, so he rebelled. Jim's mother sent him to me.

When Jim told me he couldn't write about something that he thought was completely ridiculous, I asked him how much he knew about kites. He replied, "Oh, I have seen the kites fly. Flying kites is not interesting to me."

I asked Jim if he knew that Benjamin Franklin discovered electricity through flying a kite. He knew a little about Benjamin Franklin, so this interested him. I continued my story about Benjamin Franklin. I told him Franklin was flying a homemade kite when lightning traveled down the wire to a key fastened to the kite. This created a spark. This led to Franklin's discovery of electricity.

I asked him if he had heard of Alexander Graham Bell, the man who invented the telephone. He said he had read about Alexander Graham Bell.

I told him that Alexander Graham Bell used kites to learn to fly. He was very interested in making aircraft.

We talked about beautiful kites we had seen. He was surprised that kites had uses other than being a plaything.

"Think about it. Now do you think you can write about kites?" He said that he would try. He did very well. He needed a little background before he could fulfill the assignment.

Building background for an assignment is very important. It is difficult to become excited or interested in something you know little about.

Tutoring calls on the instructor to find ways not ordinarily applied in teaching.

Oral reading is a must in working with the struggling student. So many times the student finds himself in a reading circle with several other students. He is asked to follow the reading of the other students until it is his turn to read. This is terribly boring. I would like to suggest some ways that have proven successful for teaching oral reading.

Having the student pick up the reading where a student stops. This may be in the middle of the paragraph. This keeps the student's attention.

Repeated Readings are helpful for the slow reader or non-reader. You may have the student guide you as you read. Then ask the student to read what you have read. This is slow, but it works. Perhaps it won't be necessary to do this often.

Have the student tell you about a favorite pet or game. Write as the student talks. Now, have the student read what you have written. He will be surprised that he can read his own story.

Take turns with the student. This can be done easily in tutoring. You might try this with the reading circle. You might read a paragraph and then let a student read.

We shared the reading with the student quite often when we worked with a disabled student in the summer reading class.

One summer a graduate student was having a problem with a first grader. The student entered class with the remark, "I am not going to read today." The student teacher was so intimidated that she came to me. I told her that my student was an excellent worker and would be happy to work with her. My student knew exactly what we hoped to accomplish that day. My little girl smiled and assured the graduate student that she would be happy to work with her. This freed me to take the obstinate student.

I walked into the room and said, "Good morning, how are you?" He smiled and greeted me. I said, "I am going to work with you today. Will you show me what you are reading?" He quickly opened the book and pointed to the place he was supposed to be that day. I asked, "Are you going to start the reading or shall I?" He said he would be glad to read first. Everything went smoothly.

I told his teacher that she should not bring up the event ever. She should walk into the room confident that she was the one in control. She never had a problem again.

A grandmother brought her fifth-grade grandson to Bella Vista Community Church Tutoring Program. Her grandson and his father were living with them because there had been a divorce.

Bill, the grandson, was not happy about coming to tutoring. I always gave the student a Slosson Oral Reading Test so we would have some idea of placement.

Bill was belligerent. He said that this was his playing time and he did not want to be here. I replied, "Well, I did not ask for you to come. Someone who loves you very much thinks that you are falling behind in your work. Now, if you don't want to be helped that is just fine with me. There is Adam.

His tutor is a little late. I am going to help Adam. You sit here and think about it. When I come back you can tell me whether you want help or not. If you don't want help, you can leave."

When I returned he was ready to take the test. He was assigned a tutor. He continued coming with his grandmother. His attitude was wonderful and this made his progress successful. He was cheerful and pleased with the improvement in his grades.

You have noticed that the range in age of the students needing help with reading is extensive. It is important that the material selected for reading is interesting to the individual being taught. Dolch published a number of books that were of reduced reading ability but quite interesting subjects. He had stories of dogs and horses that were interesting to adults and older students.

Another book that worked for me was Peter Jenkins, *Walk Across America*. This story is so good because it talks about the attitude of the author as he graduated from high school. He was not appreciating America, his home country. He was a good friend of the custodian of the school where he graduated. He was badmouthing America. The custodian suggested that perhaps he did not know America. Maybe he should walk across America. He should meet the people and just maybe he would change his mind. Peter thought this sounded like a good idea. So he trained with his dog for walking across America. He would not take a lot of money. He would work to cover expenses. This is a wonderful revelation.

Reader's Digest had a set of Reduced Reading Stories. These were taken from stories Reader's Digest had published in its regular edition. They had been adjusted in reading levels to help students having trouble with reading. I do not know whether they have continued doing this. The Reduced Reading Stories could be found from the first-grade to the eighth-grade level.

Games are a valuable source of learning. I like rewarding good work by playing a game with the student. Dominoes and Scrabble are excellent for reinforcing skills that have been taught.

Children have video games now. Parents buy those, but do they play the game with the child? I ask this because I really do not know. If parents do not play games with the child, the child is missing the thrill of having that parent's attention.

Our son was a math major. How could we know when we were young parents that the math games he and his dad played at the dinner table would set the background for his lifetime career. He did not memorize multiplication tables. It was not necessary.

Conclusion

Teaching, for me, was a privilege. For the most part I thoroughly enjoyed working with the students. The age did not matter. The first graders were at the beginning of learning. There was a great big world out there. They were here to learn about that world. They needed someone to "open a door" and invite them into a huge book and see what it told them. Learning to work together unselfishly, enjoying new information and testing it to see if it really worked was a thrill for both the teacher and the student.

Each grade offered more wonderful things. There were more challenging ideas, more experiments to test and a great feeling of success when they worked. The pleasure was hearing a word of praise or encouragement from the teacher. The smile on her face and the suggestion of other materials to prove that there was more to be learned made learning more interesting.

I enjoyed sharing Thomas Edison's life story with my students. I wanted them to know that one failure was not really failure. Like Edison, if whatever was tried did not work, you did not despair. You put that aside and tried something else. There was a solution, but you had to find it.

The university graduates had reached a completion and a beginning. Now they had that long sought-after degree. They had spent many years and many hours of hard work to achieve a degree. Was the challenge over? Indeed not! The challenge now was, "Where does this degree take me?"

Now job applications are in order. Many times students would return to my office saying, "There are no jobs out there!"

My reply was, "Oh, yes, there are! You just have to find them."

Then we would look at resumes and talk about methods of approach to the prospective employers. We discussed everything from personal appearance to confident attitude. You did not go in and appear rejected before you were. Then you thanked the employer for his time and asked for any other places that might need your expertise.

You do have something that you can do and you know it. You do not go after one job, but several.

I shared with you one story of a wonderfully gifted black student who knocked on my classroom door. I excused myself and answered that knock. She was beaming! She said, "I just had to tell you. I have a job!" The lucky school could not know what a jewel they had just employed.

You have to start somewhere. My son had completed his army requirement. He had his degree, so he went to an employment agency. They sent him to an engineering firm. He was a math major, not an engineering major. This company wanted to hire him for a fabulous salary.

He was frightened. He came home to talk with us. I suggested that he had to start somewhere. I said, "You must jump in somewhere. If you cannot swim you can always get out."

That beginning position led him to his wonderful career of "space scientist."

This is who we are as teachers. We are leaders in learning from the time the student enters first grade to the day he/she finds a place in our wide, wide world.